Student's Book

	Welcome to the TTSLN	page 2
1	A world of gadgets	page 4
2	Sports scene	page 14
3	Awesome animals	page 24
4	People and professions	page 34
5	Past times	page 44
6	Fruit and vegetables	page 54
7	Holiday in the city	page 64
	Festivals	page 74
	Songs bank	page 77

Carol Read • Mark Ormerod

Welcome to the Tiger Tracks Social Learning Network

Lessons 1 & 2

1 Listen and read.

Come and join the Tiger Tracks Social Learning Network! Here's what we do:
- communicate with children in other countries
- share ideas and opinions
- learn interesting content (CLIL)
- learn about different cultures
- do exciting and creative projects
- make friends and have fun

1 Hi there. My name's Lisa. I'm eleven years old. I'm from the USA. I like music and films.

Birthday: 30th September
Favourite subject: English
Favourite food: pizza

2 Listen and repeat.

1st	2nd	3rd	4th	5th	6th	7th
8th	9th	10th	11th	12th	13th	14th
15th	16th	17th	18th	19th	20th	21st
22nd	23rd	24th	25th	26th	27th	28th
29th	30th	31st				

3   Ask and say.

When's your birthday?

It's on 7th May.

2

2 Hello. I'm Duncan. I'm from Scotland. I'm twelve years old. I like old castles.

Birthday: 3rd November
Favourite subject: history
Favourite food: fish and chips

3 Hello. My name's Sita. I'm twelve years old. I'm from India. I love wild animals.

Birthday: 24th May
Favourite subject: maths
Favourite food: chicken and rice

4 Hi there! My name's Rosa. I'm from England. I'm eleven years old. I love computers and the internet.

Birthday: 18th March
Favourite subject: design and technology
Favourite food: strawberry smoothies

5 Hello everyone. I'm Steve. I'm from Australia. I'm ten years old. I like sport.

Birthday: 6th October
Favourite subject: PE
Favourite food: pasta and salad

6 Hi there. My name's Joseph. I'm from South Africa. I'm eleven years old. I love fruit and vegetables.

Birthday: 11th December
Favourite subject: science
Favourite food: fruit salad

4 Listen and say. Play *Who is it?*

He's twelve years old. His favourite subject is history.

Her birthday is on 30th September. She likes music and films.

5 Ask your friends. Tell the class.

What do you like?

What's your favourite subject?

What's your favourite food?

3

1 A world of gadgets

In this unit:

- I **name** and **describe** electronic gadgets.
- I **listen to** and **read** a biography *The father of computer science*.
- I **talk about** the frequency people do things.
- I **find out about** English and UK culture.
- I **act out** buying an electronic gadget, in a role play.
- I **read about** electronic gadgets and write a project.

Lesson 1

1 Listen and say.

Tiger Tracks SLN — POST ✓

Hi, everyone. My name's Rosa. I'm from England. In my country, lots of people use electronic gadgets – including me. I've got four of the electronic gadgets in the photos. Can you guess which ones? Can you name any other electronic gadgets?

 1    2    3

calculator   tablet   MP3 player

 4    5    6    7

headphones   video games console   webcam   stopwatch

 8    9    10

pen drive   satnav   charger

2 Listen and find out. Which electronic gadgets has Rosa got? 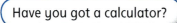 Now ask and talk about you.

Have you got a calculator?   Yes, I have.

3   Listen and do the vocabulary quiz.

You put these on your head to listen to music. What are they?

4   **INTERNET TRACKS**   Find out what the letters USB mean.

Lesson 2

4 Listen and read.

Hi, guys! Look at this advertisement for a new tablet. It does almost everything. I think it looks great! What's your opinion?

POST ✓

The Fab Tab

**It's the fabulous tablet!
It's ideal for home and school.**

READING TIP: Use the context to guess the meaning of words you don't know.

With a Fab Tab, you don't need a laptop or a computer.
A Fab Tab is small and light. You can carry it in your school bag.
A Fab Tab helps you learn fast. It's easy to use. It's lots of fun.
And guess what? If you drop it by accident, it doesn't break.

a   The camera takes great photos.
b   The calculator helps you do maths.
c   The satnav helps you learn geography.
d   The headphones help you concentrate.
e   You can use the stopwatch to time your homework.
f   You can use the MP3 player to listen to podcasts in English.
g   You can use the webcam to meet children in other countries.

I always have my Fab Tab with me. It's brilliant!

I never go to school without my Fab Tab. It's amazing!

Get a Fab Tab today!

5 Answer the questions.
1. What is the Fab Tab ideal for?
2. Where can you carry the Fab Tab?
3. What happens if you drop the Fab Tab?
4. What do the headphones help you do?
5. What can you use the MP3 player to do?

6 Play *The chain game*.

THINKING SKILLS
Evaluating

A Fab Tab is small.

A Fab Tab is small and it's easy to use.

7 Choose and say.

I want to use the camera on a Fab Tab to take great photos.

INTERNET TRACKS   Find out one difference between a tablet and a laptop.

5

Lesson 3

8 Listen to and read the story.

Hi there! This is the biography of Alan Turing. He's an early hero in computer science. His work is still important for electronic gadgets we use today. I think that's amazing! Do you agree?

POST ✓

The father of computer science

- What school subjects is Alan good at?
- What does he love doing?

1 It is 1912. Alan Turing is born in London. As a young child, Alan learns to read in three weeks and he loves numbers.

9 6 4 0 3 8 9 5 6 0 1 …
9 6 4 0 …

Come on, Alan! You don't need to learn the numbers by heart.

No, but I want to.

2 When Alan is six years old, he starts primary school. He's very good at maths. He also loves doing puzzles and secret codes.

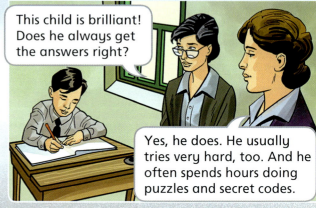

This child is brilliant! Does he always get the answers right?

Yes, he does. He usually tries very hard, too. And he often spends hours doing puzzles and secret codes.

3 One day on a picnic with his family, Alan uses maths to calculate the flight path of some bees. The bees lead Alan and his family to the honey.

Look over here! The path of the bees is like this. And there's the honey.

Mmm, delicious. Well done, Alan!

4 When Alan is thirteen, he starts secondary school. He's very good at science and maths. But the teachers aren't always happy.

You need to work hard in all subjects, not just science and maths.

And you need to spend less time doing puzzles and secret codes.

9 Read and say *True* or *False*. Correct the false sentences.

1. Alan's very bad at maths.
2. Alan loves doing puzzles and codes.
3. At secondary school, Alan works hard at all subjects.
4. Alan studies English at Oxford University.
5. The 'Turing machine' is a way of calculating numbers.
6. Alan develops one of the first computers at Cambridge University.

Think about it!

Is it important to follow your interests at home and at school?

How do you follow your interests at home and at school?

5 When Alan leaves school, he studies maths at Cambridge University. He develops a way of calculating numbers. It's called the 'Turing machine'.

Congratulations, Turing! This is brilliant work.

Thank you.

6 After university, Alan works at Bletchley Park, a big house in the countryside. He works with a team of people to crack the famous secret code, Enigma.

Oh dear! We can never solve this code. There are millions of possibilities.

But we can't stop trying now. We need to work hard and be patient.

7 One day, Alan suddenly has an idea. It helps the team to crack the Enigma code.

Look! I think the code works like this.

You're right!

Well done, Alan!

8 Later, Alan develops one of the first computers at Manchester University. He also works on 'artificial intelligence' and secret codes.

Here's the computer printout and my notes to solve the problem.

That's fantastic, Alan. You're a genius!

9 Alan Turing's work on computer science, secret codes and artificial intelligence is important for electronic gadgets that we use today, like laptops and tablets. What a brilliant achievement for a boy who loves puzzles and secret codes at school!

Do you know...?
The 'Turing award' is an annual prize for computer science. In the UK, schools sometimes have code-breaking competitions to try to find the next Alan Turing.

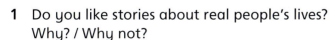

10 Ask and say.
1 Do you like stories about real people's lives? Why? / Why not?
2 Do you think Alan is a genius?
3 What's your favourite part of the story?
4 Can you name other people who are famous for their work in science or technology?

Everyday phrases: learn and use!

Come on!

Look over here!

Well done!

You're right!

GRAMMAR TRACKS

Lesson 4

11 Listen and read. Say the gadgets they use.

Lucy: I **usually** use my laptop to write emails. I **sometimes** use my tablet or my mobile phone to send messages. I **often** listen to music on my MP3 player. I **always** use my headphones. I **never** use a stopwatch in the gym.

Zak: I **usually** use my tablet to read the newspaper. I **always** use my mobile phone to call my friends. I **never** use a laptop. I **sometimes** use a digital camera. I **often** use my headphones. I **never** use a calculator to do maths.

12   Say and ask.

 This person always uses headphones. Who is it?

It's Lucy!

13 Listen, repeat and learn.

Adverbs of frequency

I / You / We / They	always usually often	use	a satnav. a tablet. a calculator.
He / She	sometimes never	use**s**	a stopwatch. a webcam.

never — sometimes — often / usually — always
0% ———————————————— 100%

Does	he / she	use a tablet?

Yes,	he / she	always usually often sometimes	do**es**.
No,		never	

14 Be a grammar detective!
Look at page 7 in the AB.

When do we use adverbs of frequency?

Where do we put adverbs of frequency in sentences?

Where do we put adverbs of frequency in answers to questions?

Can you find two adverbs of frequency in the story?

 FAST TRACK GRAMMAR *Write five sentences using adverbs of frequency.*

Lesson 5

15 Listen and identify /tʃ/ and /dʒ/. Count and say.

Jamie always chats and eats cheese and jam when he uses his stopwatch in the gym.

Charlie loves gadgets and always uses his digital camera and charger in geography.

16 Listen and correct the sentences.

Things we do on Saturday

	never	sometimes	often	usually	always
Ben	books	shopping	TV	football	computer
Lyn	TV	football	computer	shopping	books
Sam	TV	shopping	computer	football	books
Jo	books	football	TV	shopping	computer

17 Play *Who am I thinking about?*

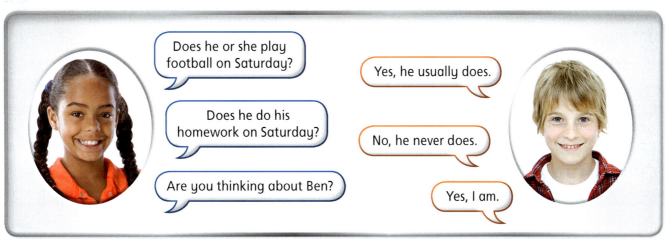

Does he or she play football on Saturday?
Yes, he usually does.
Does he do his homework on Saturday?
No, he never does.
Are you thinking about Ben?
Yes, I am.

18 Talk about you and your friends.

I sometimes watch TV on Saturday.
David always plays football on Saturday.

 FAST TRACK GRAMMAR Write five sentences about what you and a friend do on Saturday.

There are many cities in England with universities. Oxford and Cambridge are famous all over the world.

POST ✓

Lesson 6

19 Listen and read.

OXFORD AND CAMBRIDGE

Oxford and Cambridge are cities in the south of England. They are famous for their universities. There are lots of things to see and do in both cities.

In Oxford, the dining room of Christ Church College is Hogwarts Hall in the Harry Potter films. Magdalen College has got a large deer park.

At the Pitt Rivers Museum, you can see traditional costumes.

In Cambridge, you can walk in a beautiful park by the River Cam. The Botanic Garden has got a glasshouse with carnivorous plants and a tropical rainforest. At the Fitzwilliam Museum, you can see ancient Egyptian mummies.

Every year there is a boat race on the River Thames in London between students from Oxford and Cambridge Universities. In England the race is always on TV. Many people support either Oxford or Cambridge. The race is often exciting and the winners are always happy.

What famous cities are there in your country?

20 Read and guess. Listen and say the answers.

England is part of the UK. Here's a fun culture quiz about England. Can you do it?

POST ✓

Culture quiz time: *England*

1. What's the capital of England?   a) Oxford   b) London   c) Manchester
2. Who is on every English stamp?   a) Shakespeare   b) the Prime Minister   c) the Queen
3. What colour are English post boxes?   a) yellow   b) blue   c) red
4. What's the name of the river in London?   a) The Thames   b) The Severn   c) The Cam
5. What's the favourite food of England?   a) fish and chips   b) chicken curry   c) roast beef
6. What's the most popular country for a holiday?   a) Spain   b) Italy   c) France

POST ✓

I love shopping with my family and friends – especially for electronic gadgets. Here are some facts about shopping in English towns.

Lesson 7

21 **Listen and read. Say *True* or *False*.**

1 The main shops are usually in the High Street.
2 There are always big shopping centres.
3 You can never go shopping on Sunday.
4 There are sometimes corner shops in residential streets.
5 Corner shops often stay open very late and at the weekend.
6 Supermarkets always stay open all night.

Everyday chit-chat

 How to buy an electronic gadget

22 **Listen and repeat.**

   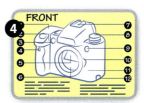

pounds   pence   receipt   instructions

23 **Listen and read. Repeat.**

Woman: Hello there. Can I help you?
Rosa: Oh, yes, please. I need a new charger for my digital camera.
Woman: Right. Come this way, please. All the chargers for digital cameras are over here.
Rosa: Oh, great. I think this is the one I need. How much is it?
Woman: This one is twenty-one pounds and fifty pence.
Rosa: Right. Here you are. Five… ten … twenty-one pounds and fifty pence exactly.
Woman: Lovely. Thank you. Here's your receipt. And the instructions are in the packet.
Rosa: Thank you very much for your help.
Woman: You're welcome. Don't forget your camera!
Rosa: Oh, thanks! Goodbye.

24 **Do a role play.**

CLIL
Social Science

Lesson 8

 25 Listen and read.

 Hi there! I love using electronic gadgets but I also love riding my bike and doing sport. Here's an interesting web article about children and electronic gadgets. Do you agree with it? POST ✓

How often do you use electronic gadgets?

Children often use electronic gadgets at home and at school. These include laptops, tablets, video games consoles and mobile phones.

But if you always use electronic gadgets and never do anything else, you need to change your lifestyle. There are many positive things, or pros, about electronic gadgets. But there are also some negative things, or cons, too.

What are the pros?
Electronic gadgets:
- improve your keyboard skills.
- make you more creative.
- help you find out about the world.
- help you learn school subjects.

What are the cons?
Some children use electronic gadgets for seven hours a day, or fifty hours a week. This means that you:
- often sit in front of a screen for a long time.
- don't have time for exercise and outdoor activities.
- only play video and computer games.
- sometimes find it hard to concentrate on school work.

Conclusion
It's important to keep a balance. Electronic gadgets are fun and help you learn but you need to find time to do exercise and other activities as well.

26 Answer the questions.
1 What do electronic gadgets improve?
2 What do they help you find out about?
3 What do they help you learn?
4 How often do children sometimes use electronic gadgets?
5 What don't you have time for?
6 What do you sometimes find hard to do?

27 Play *Pro or Con?*

 They make you more creative. — Pro!
You don't have time for exercise. — Con!

THINKING SKILLS
Evaluating

28 Think and say.
Do you and your friends use electronic gadgets?
What's your opinion of the pros and cons?

My words to remember
pro   con   lifestyle   creative   skill   concentrate

 **INTERNET TRACKS** Find out one more pro or con of children using electronic gadgets.

Project: Electronic gadget survey

29 **Listen and read.**

 Look at my electronic gadget survey report. Who never uses an MP3 player in my family? Who uses all the gadgets? POST ✓

Electronic gadget survey report

The aim of my survey is to find out about electronic gadgets grown-ups in my family use. This report is about my mother, my father, my grandfather, and my aunt.

My mum always uses her mobile phone. She never uses a tablet or a video games console. She usually uses the satnav in the car. She sometimes listens to music on her MP3 player.

My dad often uses his mobile phone. He usually uses his tablet to write emails. He always uses his video games console and the satnav. He never listens to an MP3 player.

My grandad sometimes uses his mobile phone and his video games console. He often uses a tablet and an MP3 player. He never uses a satnav.

My aunt always uses her tablet. She often uses a video games console and the satnav in the car. She usually uses her mobile phone and listens to music on her MP3 player.

By Rosa

30 Plan your project.

1. Choose who to ask.
2. Prepare a questionnaire.
3. Ask the questions in your survey.
4. Prepare and write your project.

You can present your project in this way.

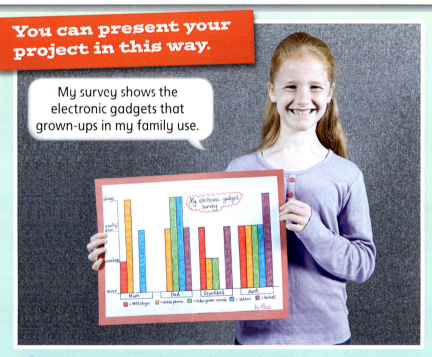

My survey shows the electronic gadgets that grown-ups in my family use.

→ AB page 12

Do the Unit 1 Review and self-assessment (Activity Book page 12). Complete your *Progress Journal* for Unit 1.

2 Sports scene

In this unit:

- I **name** and **describe** sports.
- I **listen to** and **read** a travel story on a blog *The survival guide*.
- I **talk about** what people are doing.
- I **find out about** Australian and UK culture.
- I **act out** asking for information about sports classes, in a role play.
- I **read about** exercise and write a project.

Lesson 1

1 Listen and say.

Tiger Tracks SLN   POST ✓

Hi, everyone. My name's Steve. I'm from Australia. In my country, many people love sport. Two of Australia's favourite sports are in the list below. Can you guess which they are? Can you name any other sports?

1 badminton

2 surfing

3 snowboarding

4 kayaking

5 cricket

6 cycling

7 bowling

8 sailing

9 scuba diving

10 rugby

2 Listen and find out. Which sports does Steve like? Which are Australia's favourite sports? Now ask and talk about you.

Do you like badminton?   *Yes, I do. It's fun.*

3 Listen and do the vocabulary quiz.

You wear a special suit and dive under the sea. What sport is it?

14 **INTERNET TRACKS** Find out the name of a type of football people only play in Australia.

Lesson 2

4 Listen and read.

Hi, everyone! Here's a leaflet about holiday tours in Australia. There's something for everyone. I hope you can visit Australia one day. ☺

POST ✓

Australia – land of sport, nature and fun.
Whatever you want to do, we've got the tour for you!

READING TIP: Use the headings to predict the content.

Sports tour
On this tour, we see famous Australian sports teams play cricket and rugby. We go sailing and surfing at the seaside. We also go scuba diving off the famous Great Barrier Reef.

These men are playing cricket.

City tour
On this tour, we visit the beautiful city of Sydney. We visit the famous Sydney Opera House and walk across the Sydney Harbour Bridge. We also visit the Australian Reptile Park – it's famous for the big lake full of crocodiles.

These girls are looking at Sydney Harbour.

Rainforest tour

This family is walking in the rainforest.

On this tour, we discover the natural beauty and wildlife of Australian rainforests. We see giant trees, exotic plants, rivers and waterfalls. We also discover animals, such as koalas and possums, which live in Australia.

Outback tour
On this tour, we drive across the Australian outback. We visit the famous Uluru and learn about the Aborigines, the first people to live in Australia. We see Australian animals, such as kangaroos and dingos.

These people are visiting Uluru.

5 Answer the questions.
1. What famous sports do you watch on the sports tour?
2. What famous building do you visit on the city tour?
3. What animals do you discover on the rainforest tour?
4. Who do you learn about on the outback tour?

6 Play *The association game*.

THINKING SKILLS Associating

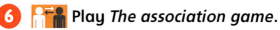

You walk across a bridge.

It's the city tour!

7 Choose and say.

I want to go on the rainforest tour to see koalas.

INTERNET TRACKS Find out the name of one more Australian animal.

Lesson 3

8 Listen to and read the story.

Hi there! This is a travel story about an Australian family. They go on a bike ride in the school holidays to raise money for a children's charity. Natalie is eleven years old and her brother, Jack, is ten. Here are extracts from Natalie's blog.

POST ✓

The survival guide

- What's the disaster?
- Who can help?

1 This is our route from Adelaide to Sydney. It's about 1,400 kilometres. We've got everything on our bikes – food, water, clothes, sleeping bags and a tent. My little brother Jack's got his favourite book, *The survival guide*. We're excited and nervous. Can we do it?

2 Day 1 – In this photo we're cycling in the countryside and looking at a kangaroo. The bikes are heavy and Jack's complaining that it's difficult. When we stop, I help Mum and Dad put up the tent. Jack reads *The survival guide*.

3 Day 3 – It's freezing cold in the night and there's ice on the tent. The day is windy and we cycle slowly. In this photo we're eating sandwiches in the Koala Café. Jack's reading *The survival guide* and complaining that he hasn't got a hot lunch.

4 Day 6 – This is our first rest day. We're in Waikerie – 174 kilometres from Adelaide. We're staying in a hotel. I'm happy because I can have a shower and sleep in a real bed. Jack's reading *The survival guide* and complaining that this isn't a real adventure.

9 Answer the questions.

1. How far is it from Adelaide to Sydney?
2. What do they see on Day 1?
3. Why is Natalie happy on their first rest day?
4. What stings Mum's ankle?
5. How many days does the bike ride take?
6. How much money do they raise for charity?

Tiger Time Values — Think about it!

Is it important to help other people?

How do you help other people?

5

Day 25 – We cycle up to Mount Victoria in the rain. Mount Victoria is a village in the mountains. It's spectacular! In this photo we're having a hot drink in a café. Mum, Dad and I are chatting and Jack's reading *The survival guide* (again).

6

Day 28 – Disaster! There's a scorpion in the tent. The scorpion stings Mum's ankle. Luckily Jack's got *The survival guide*. Jack washes the poison away with soap. He puts Mum's ankle in cold water. He makes Mum lie down with her heart above the sting. He uses a bandage to stop the poison spreading.

7

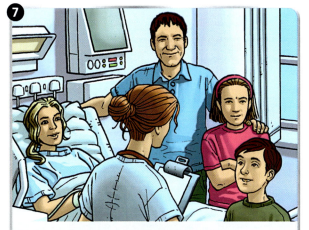

Here we are at the hospital. The nurse is saying 'well done' to Jack. Thank goodness for *The survival guide!* My little brother is a hero.

8

Day 30 – The last day of the bike ride. We're in Sydney. Mum's ankle is in a bandage. She's riding on the back of Dad's bike. Lots of people are waiting to welcome us. What a journey!

Do you know...?
Many people in countries like Australia and the UK do sport to raise money for charity. It's a popular way to help people and have fun.

9

FAMILY RAISES 10,000 DOLLARS FOR CHILDREN'S CHARITY

This is a photo from the newspaper. Mum's better now, thanks to Jack. He's still reading *The survival guide* – but I don't mind now.

10 Ask and say.
1 Do you like travel stories? Why? / Why not?
2 Do you think the bike ride is easy or difficult?
3 What's your favourite part of the story?
4 Do you want to do sport to raise money for charity?

Everyday phrases: learn and use!

It's freezing cold.

It's spectacular!

Thank goodness!

What a journey!

GRAMMAR TRACKS

Lesson 4

11 Look, listen and read. Say the differences.

Cycling

Cycling is a great sport but it's important to be safe and respect people around you.

THE GOOD CYCLIST

- She**'s wearing** a helmet.
- She**'s wearing** a brightly-coloured jacket.
- She**'s cycling** on the road.
- She**'s looking** to see who's coming.
- She**'s listening** for traffic.

THE BAD CYCLIST

- He **isn't wearing** a helmet.
- He **isn't wearing** a brightly-coloured jacket.
- He**'s cycling** on the pavement.
- He **isn't paying** attention.
- He**'s listening** to music on his MP3 player.

12 Play *Good or bad!*

 I'm wearing a helmet.

Good!

13 Listen, repeat and learn.

Present continuous tense

I**'m**		a brightly-coloured jacket.
He**'s** / She**'s**	wear**ing**	
You**'re** / We**'re** / They**'re**		helmets.

I**'m** not		on the road.
He / She is**n't**	cycl**ing**	
You / We / They are**n't**		on the pavement.

Are you	play**ing** cricket?	Yes,	I am.	No,	I**'m** not.
Is he / she	surf**ing**?		he / she is.		he / she isn**'t**.
Are we / they	kayak**ing**?		we / they are.		we / they are**n't**.

14 Be a grammar detective!
Look at page 17 in the AB.

When do we use the present continuous?

How do we make the present continuous?

Can you find three examples of the present continuous tense in the story?

FAST TRACK GRAMMAR *Write five sentences using the present continuous tense.*

Lesson 5

 Listen and identify /aɪ/ and /eɪ/. Count and say.

Eileen likes kayaking, scuba diving, cycling, ice skating and playing table tennis.

Adrian likes sailing, skateboarding, rollerblading and riding a horse.

 Listen and correct the answers.

 Play *Yes or No!*

Is it a boy?

So it's a girl. Is she wearing a red T-shirt?

OK. Is she playing badminton?

And is she wearing a yellow T-shirt?

Is she number 12?

No, it isn't.

No, she isn't.

Yes, she is.

Yes, she is.

Yes, she is.

 Mime and guess.

Are you kayaking?

No, I'm not.

Are you bowling?

Yes, I am.

 FAST TRACK GRAMMAR *Write five sentences about what people are doing in activity 16.*

My country is famous for water sports! How many of these water sports do you know? Can you identify the water sports in the photos?

POST ✓

Cult

Lesson 6

19 Listen and read.

Water sports in Australia

Australia has got many rivers and beautiful beaches. It's also got a good climate. For this reason it's a perfect place for water sports!

Windsurfing and kitesurfing are popular sports. To do these sports you use a surfboard with a large sail, or a surfboard with a large kite, to ride the waves.

Water polo is a team sport. There are six players and a goalkeeper on each team. Players swim, pass the ball and score goals.

Snorkelling is the perfect way to discover the world under the sea. You can see the corals and multi-coloured fish of the Great Barrier Reef.

Waterskiing is a popular sport. You wear skis and a lifejacket. A motor boat pulls you through the water very fast.

White water rafting is an exciting way to discover the rivers and tropical rainforests of Australia. You wear a helmet and a lifejacket and you paddle in a raft with six or eight other people.

What water sports do people do in your country?

20 Read and guess. Listen and say the answers.

Here's a cool culture quiz about Australia. Can you guess the answers?

POST ✓

Culture quiz time: Australia

1. What's the capital of Australia? a) Sydney b) Perth c) Canberra
2. How many square kilometres is Australia? a) 3.3 million b) 5.5 million c) 7.7 million
3. Which two animals are the symbols of Australia? a) the kangaroo and the koala b) the kangaroo and the emu c) the koala and the emu
4. What's the popular name for the Sydney Harbour Bridge? a) the coat hanger b) the rainbow c) the hoop
5. How high is Uluru? a) 150 metres b) 250 metres c) 350 metres
6. There are more than 20 million people in Australia. How many sheep are there? a) 10 million b) 50 million c) 100 million

The only water sport I do is swimming! My favourite sport is football. These days football is very popular in the UK with girls as well as boys.

Lesson 7

 Listen and read. Say *True* or *False*.

1. The name of the national stadium in England is Wembley.
2. The main English national football team colour is blue.
3. Manchester United is a popular club in the south of England.
4. Chelsea, Arsenal, Tottenham Hotspur and West Ham United are all clubs from Manchester.
5. The top professional teams in England play in the Premier League.
6. There are some Spanish players in the English professional leagues.

Everyday chit-chat

 How to find out about sports classes

 Listen and repeat.

coach   sports kit   locker   changing room

 Listen and read. Repeat.

Rosa: Good afternoon. I'd like to find out about football coaching.
Man: Can you play football? Or are you a beginner?
Rosa: I'm a beginner.
Man: Well, we have football coaching for beginners once a week. It's after school every Thursday at 5.30. The coach is a player at the football club.
Rosa: That's perfect. How much does it cost?
Man: The coaching is free. But you need to buy your own sports kit. There are lockers in the changing room.
Rosa: Can I start on Thursday?
Man: Yes, of course. It's Thursday today!
Rosa: Wow! Is it really? Thank you.

  Do a role play.

Science

Lesson 8

25 Listen and read.

 Hi there! We all know that exercise is good for us. But do you know about the three different kinds of exercise we need to do? Read on … and enjoy! ☺ POST ✓

Exercise is healthy and cool

When you do exercise, you breathe fast and your heart pumps blood around your body. The blood carries oxygen from your lungs to your muscles. Your muscles help your joints to move.

With regular exercise, you:
- build strong muscles
- keep a healthy weight
- sleep well at night
- feel good about yourself
- feel less worried or stressed
- feel ready to learn at school

There are three main kinds of exercise:

Aerobic exercise
Aerobic exercise needs lots of oxygen. It makes you breathe fast. Aerobic exercise is good for your heart. Swimming and tennis are examples of aerobic exercise. When you run, skip and jump in the playground, that's aerobic exercise, too.

Strength training
Strength training is good for your muscles. Strong muscles support your joints and stop you getting hurt. Cycling and rowing are examples of strength training. When you do handstands in the playground, that's strength training, too.

Flexibility training
Flexibility training helps your body stretch and bend. It is good for your muscles and joints. Gymnastics and judo are examples of flexibility training. When you touch your toes, that's flexibility training, too.

To stay fit and healthy, it's good to do all three kinds of exercise.

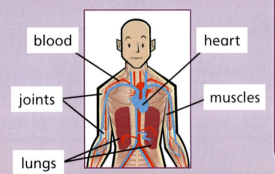

blood | heart | joints | muscles | lungs

26 Read and correct the sentences.
1. Your muscles pump blood around your body.
2. With regular exercise, you don't sleep at night.
3. Aerobic exercise makes you breathe slowly.
4. Strong muscles support your lungs.
5. It's good to do one kind of exercise.

27  Play *Say a sentence!*

 This is good for your heart.

Aerobic exercise!

28 Think and say.
What's your favourite kind of exercise?
What do you do to get aerobic exercise, strength training and flexibility training?

THINKING SKILLS
Categorising

My words to remember
muscle   heart   oxygen   blood   lungs   joints

  Find out approximately how many muscles there are in the human body.

Project: Do I get enough exercise?

29 **Listen and read.**

Look at my project on ways I get exercise. What exercise do I do on school days? What exercise do I do at the weekend? POST ✓

Do I get enough exercise?

In this photo I'm walking the dog with my sister.

Every week I get lots of exercise. From Monday to Friday, I walk to school and back home. It takes fifteen minutes each way. At school, we have PE twice a week for an hour on Monday and Thursday. We do gym and we also play football and rugby. At break time, I play football and tag in the playground with my friends. After school, I go to swimming lessons once a week on Friday. I'm also a member of a club where I play badminton on Saturday. At the weekend, I walk the dog and I go jogging with my dad. On Sunday, we cycle in the park.

Here my friends are playing football in the school playground.

I think I get about eleven hours of exercise every week. When I do exercise, I feel good about myself. I get hungry and thirsty and I sleep well.

By Duncan

30 Plan your project.

1. Think of all the ways you get exercise.
2. Complete your exercise diary.
3. Ask a friend or someone in your family to take photos.
4. Prepare and write your project.

You can present your project in this way.

Every week I get lots of exercise. In this photo I'm cycling in the park with my dad.

➡ AB page 22

Do the Unit 2 Review and self-assessment (Activity Book page 22). Complete your *Progress Journal* for Unit 2.

3 Awesome animals

AIMS

In this unit:
- I **name** and **describe** animals.
- I **listen to** and **read** a traditional story *How the tiger got its stripes*.
- I **compare** animals and people.
- I **find out about** Indian and UK culture.
- I **act out** buying tickets, in a role play.
- I **read about** endangered animals and write a project.

Lesson 1

1 Listen and say.

Tiger Tracks SLN POST ✓

Hi, everyone. My name's Sita. I'm from India. In my country, we've got some awesome animals. Can you guess which of these animals live in India? Do you know any other animals which live in India?

1 rhino — 2 deer — 3 red panda

4 hippo — 5 panther — 6 snow leopard — 7 buffalo

8 eagle — 9 baboon — 10 flamingo

2 Ask and say your opinion. Listen and check. Which animals live in India?

- Do rhinos live in India?
- Yes, I think so.
- I'm not sure.
- No, they don't.

3 Listen and do the vocabulary quiz.

It's got soft, black fur. It's fierce. It runs very fast. What is it?

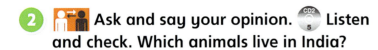   Find out the names of three more animals that live in India.

Lesson 2

4 **Listen and read.**

 Here's a website where you can find out more about wildlife in India!

POST ✓

Wildlife in India

India has got hundreds of different mammals and reptiles, and thousands of birds. There are more than one hundred national parks in India which protect wild animals.

Some national parks are near rivers and forests. It is hot in the summer and cold in the winter. There is also a monsoon season when it rains a lot. In these parks, you can see elephants, tigers and baboons. You can also see flamingos, deer, red pandas and buffalo. There are also rhinos and hippos. Rhinos are bigger than hippos, but hippos are fiercer.

READING TIP: The first sentence of each paragraph tells you what the paragraph is about.

Some national parks are in the mountains. There is lots of snow and it is freezing cold. There is no monsoon season and the summer is short. In these parks, you can see bears, eagles and mountain deer. You can also see wolves, foxes and the rare snow leopard. Snow leopards have got black or brown spots. They are smaller than tigers. Snow leopards live on their own and they do not roar.

THINKING SKILLS
Comparing and contrasting

5 Answer the questions.
1. How many national parks are there in India?
2. Where can you see baboons and flamingos?
3. Where can you see eagles and wolves?
4. Where is there a monsoon season?
5. Where is there lots of snow?

6 Play *The memory game*.

Where can you see baboons?

In parks near rivers and forests!

7 Choose and say.

I want to go to a park in the mountains because I want to see a snow leopard.

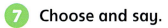 **INTERNET TRACKS** Find out the name of a national park in India.

25

Lesson 3

8 Listen to and read the story.

There are many stories about animals in India. This is a traditional story about how the tiger got its stripes. Check it out and let me know what you think. Enjoy! ☺

POST ✓

How the tiger got its stripes

- Why is the tiger curious?
- What is the man's trick?

1 A long time ago, in the days when animals can speak, tigers are white or brown but they haven't got stripes. Then one day something happens to change this forever.

2 A tiger walks to the edge of the forest. A man is eating his lunch by a rice field. An enormous buffalo is eating grass nearby. The tiger creeps up to the buffalo.

"Don't be scared. I'm not hungry. I'm curious. You're bigger and stronger than the man. Why do you work for him?"

"The man is more intelligent than I am."

"What is intelligence? And where does the man get it from?"

"I don't know. Why don't you ask him?"

3 The tiger leaps over to the man. The man stands up. He's shaking with fear.

"What is intelligence? Where do you get it from? Please can you share it with me."

"Intelligence is very precious. I don't want to share it with you."

"Are you sure? I'm feeling hungry …"

4 The man is worried. He thinks quickly.

"My intelligence is at home. Wait here and I can get it. Don't come with me because people in my village are scared of tigers."

"Alright. But make sure you come back. Or tomorrow I may be hungrier …"

"I don't want to leave my buffalo with a hungry tiger. Please can I tie you to this banana tree?"

9 Read and say *True* or *False*. Correct the false sentences.

1. The man is stronger than the buffalo.
2. The man is more intelligent than the buffalo.
3. The man ties the tiger to an apple tree.
4. The man and his son bring lots of wood.
5. The tiger cools his fur in the river.
6. The black stripes are from the fire.

Tiger Time Values
Think about it!

Is it important to be kind to animals?
In what ways are you kind to animals?

5 The tiger wants the man's intelligence so much that he agrees. The man ties the tiger to the banana tree with thick rope.

6 Later, the man returns with his son and lots of dry straw.

7 The man and his son lay the straw around the tiger and set it on fire. The tiger breaks the rope and leaps away.

8 The tiger races to the river. He swims in the water and cools his fur.

9 And this is the story of how the tiger got its stripes. It's also the reason why tigers never trust people!

Do you know...?
A tiger's stripes are unique – like a person's finger prints! Stripes also help tigers to hide in forests.

---

10 Ask and say.

1. Do you think the story is true? Why? / Why not?
2. Do you like the story? Why? / Why not?
3. What's your favourite part of the story?
4. Is the man intelligent or cruel?

Everyday phrases: learn and use!

Are you sure?

Alright.

Yes, of course it is.

That's better.

GRAMMAR TRACKS

Lesson 4

11 Listen and read. Say which animal is Asian or African.

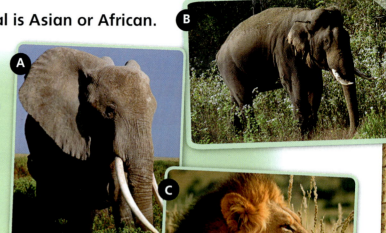

Asian or African?

The African elephant is **bigger** and **heavier** than the Asian elephant. Some people also say that it is **stronger**. The African elephant is **taller** than the Asian elephant and it's got **longer** legs. The Asian elephant has got **smaller** ears than the African elephant and its tusks are **shorter**.

The Asian lion is **smaller** and **lighter** than the African lion. The male has got a **shorter**, **darker** mane. The African lion is **stronger** and **heavier** than the Asian lion. Some people also say that it is **fiercer**. The male has got a **longer**, **thicker** mane.

12  Play *Which animal?*

"This elephant is bigger!"

"It's the African elephant!"

13 Listen, repeat and learn.

Comparative adjectives

I'm	tall.
You're	short.
He's	strong.
She's	big.
It's	heavy.
They're	intelligent.

I'm	tall**er**		you.
You're	short**er**		me.
He's	strong**er**	**than**	the boy.
She's	big**g**er		the man.
It's	heav**i**er		the buffalo.
They're	**more** intelligent		the tiger.

I've	got	short**er**	hair.

He's / She's	got	fair**er** hair.
It's		long**er** tusks.

14 Be a grammar detective!
Look at page 27 in the AB.

When do we use comparative adjectives?
How do we make comparative adjectives?

Can you find two comparative adjectives in the story?

FAST TRACK GRAMMAR Write five sentences using comparative adjectives.

Lesson 5

15 Listen and identify /ə/. Count and say.

 My sist*er*'s old*er* th*a*n my broth*er* *a*nd she's got long*er*, straight*er* hair.

 My moth*er*'s tall*er* than my fath*er* and she's got short*er*, fair*er* hair.

16 Listen and say *True* or *False*.

Lia
I'm 12 years old.
I'm 1.50 metres tall. I've got long, straight hair.

Tom
I'm 11 years old.
I'm 1.45 metres tall.
I've got short, dark hair.

Spike
I'm 10 years old.
I'm 1.40 metres tall.
I've got short, fair hair.

Jen
I'm 13 years old. I'm 1.60 metres tall. I've got long, curly hair.

17 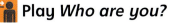 Play *Who are you?*

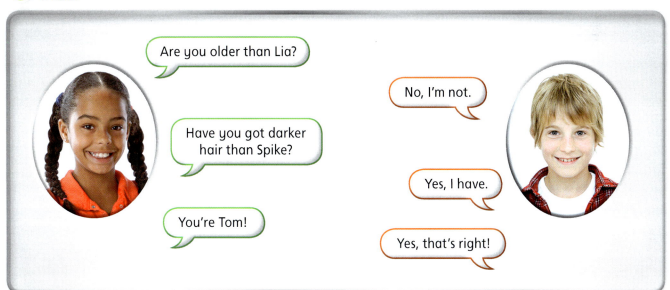

Are you older than Lia?

No, I'm not.

Have you got darker hair than Spike?

Yes, I have.

You're Tom!

Yes, that's right!

18 Talk about you and your friends.

I'm older than Kate.
I've got bigger hands than David!

 FAST TRACK GRAMMAR   *Write five sentences comparing yourself and a friend.*

POST ✓

In my country we've got many famous buildings. My favourite is the Taj Mahal. It's awesome!

Cult

Lesson 6

19 Listen and read.

The Taj Mahal: A wonder of the world

The Taj Mahal is one of the seven wonders of the world. It is a monument to a love story in the 17th century.

The Emperor of India and his queen have a long and happy marriage.

When the queen dies, the Emperor is very sad and builds the Taj Mahal in her memory.

The Taj Mahal takes 20,000 workers and 1,000 elephants about 22 years to build.

The Taj Mahal is made of white marble and decorated with 28 varieties of precious and semi-precious stones. The Taj Mahal appears pink in the early morning, white during the day and golden in the evening. When the moon is out, it appears blue.

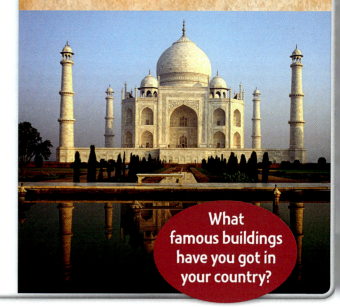

What famous buildings have you got in your country?

20 Read and guess. Listen and say the answers.

POST ✓

Now it's my turn to give you a culture quiz about India. Are you ready?

Culture quiz time: India

1. What's the capital of India?   a) Kolkata   b) New Delhi   c) Bangalore
2. What's the national animal of India?   a) the tiger   b) the elephant   c) the lion
3. Which language do many people speak?   a) French   b) English   c) Spanish
4. How many official languages are there?   a) 2   b) 22   c) 220
5. What's the favourite drink of India?   a) coffee   b) tea   c) milk
6. What's the name of India's film industry?   a) Dollywood   b) Hollywood   c) Bollywood

30

We've got many famous buildings in England, too. Blenheim Palace is amazing!

POST ✓

Lesson 7

21 **Listen and read. Say *True* or *False*.**

1. Blenheim Palace is near the city of Oxford.
2. It is the home of the Queen of England.
3. The palace is set in five square kilometres of park and gardens.
4. There is a secret garden and a magnificent lake.
5. Blenheim Palace has got one hundred rooms.
6. There are about half a million visitors to Blenheim Palace every year.

Everyday chit-chat

 How to buy tickets to visit a famous building

22 **Listen and repeat.**

ticket   change   plan   souvenir shop

23 **Listen and read. Repeat.**

Man: Next, please. How can I help you?
Rosa: I'd like three tickets to visit the castle and gardens, please.
Man: Is that for adults or children? Tickets for children under sixteen are cheaper.
Rosa: Oh, thanks. It's for one adult and two children, please.
Man: Right. That's 42 pounds in total, please.
Rosa: Here you are.
Man: Thank you. Here's your change – eight pounds – and your tickets. You show your tickets to the lady over there.
Rosa: Oh, right. Thank you.
Man: And this is a plan of the castle and gardens. It shows you the route to follow. It also shows you where the souvenir shop, café and toilets are. The castle closes at half past five and the gardens close at six o'clock.
Rosa: Oh no! But it's four o'clock now. Come on. Let's hurry!
Man: Enjoy your visit.

24   **Do a role play.**

Natural Science

Lesson 8

25 Listen and read.

Hi there! In India, animals such as rhinos, tigers and snow leopards are in danger. There are thousands of other endangered animals in countries all over the world. Here's a web page which explains the reasons and gives facts about some endangered animals. I hope you find it interesting. POST ✓

Endangered animals

Red Alert!

An endangered animal is an animal in danger of extinction. There are four main reasons why animals are endangered:

1 GLOBAL WARMING
The Earth is getting hotter. It is harder for animals to find the food and water that they need.

2 POLLUTION
The Earth, rivers and seas are polluted by chemicals and rubbish. Animals catch diseases and die.

3 LOSS OF HABITAT
Animals lose their homes when people cut down forests to build farms or roads. They also lose their source of food and water.

4 HUNTING AND POACHING
People hunt and poach wild animals for their skins, horns or tusks, or to sell them as exotic pets.

 Mountain gorillas live in Africa. There are about 800 in the world today. Gorillas are endangered because of loss of habitat, poaching and hunting baby gorillas to sell as exotic pets.

 Polar bears live in the Arctic. There are about 20,000 in the world today. Polar bears are endangered because of global warming and pollution.

 Tigers live in Asia. There are about 4,000 in the world today. Tigers are endangered because of loss of habitat, global warming, poaching and hunting for their skins.

 Giant pandas live in China. There are about 2,000 in the world today. Giant pandas are endangered because of loss of habitat and pollution.

 Indian rhinos live in Asia. There are about 3,000 in the world today. Indian rhinos are endangered because of hunting and poaching for their valuable horns.

 Snow leopards live in Asia. There are about 5,000 in the world today. Snow leopards are endangered because of loss of habitat, hunting and poaching for their skins.

26 Answer the questions.
Which animals are endangered because of …
1 loss of habitat?   3 pollution?
2 global warming?   4 hunting and poaching?

THINKING SKILLS
Categorising

27 Play *Question challenge*.

Where do polar bears live?

In the Arctic. How many tigers are there in the world today?

About four thousand. Why are Indian rhinos endangered? …

28 Think and say.
Are there endangered animals in your country? Why are they in danger?

My words to remember
endangered   habitat   pollution
global warming   hunting   poaching

INTERNET TRACKS   Find out if chimpanzees are an endangered animal.

Project: An endangered animal

29 **Listen and read.**

Look at my project about the red squirrel. Why are red squirrels endangered? How many are there in the UK today? POST ✓

An endangered animal

My favourite endangered animal is the red squirrel. Red squirrels live in the trees in woods and parks. They are red or brown and have got white fur on their chests. They eat nuts and seeds. Red squirrels are shy and live on their own.

Red squirrels are endangered because of loss of habitat, disease and road traffic. They are also in danger from grey squirrels. Red squirrels are smaller than grey squirrels but they have got longer ears and tails. Grey squirrels are heavier and stronger than red squirrels. Grey squirrels are hungrier and eat red squirrels' food. Grey squirrels also live longer than red squirrels. There are about three million grey squirrels in the UK today but there are only about 140,000 red squirrels.

By Rosa

30 Plan your project.

1. Choose an endangered animal.

2. Find out about the animal.

3. Why is the animal endangered?

4. Prepare and write your project.

You can present your project in this way.

Red squirrels live in the trees in woods and parks.

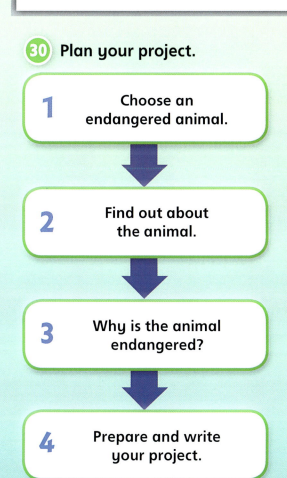

➡ AB page 32

Do the Unit 3 Review and self-assessment (Activity Book page 32). Complete your *Progress Journal* for Unit 3.

People and professions

In this unit:

- I **name** and **describe** professions.
- I **listen to** and **read** a historical story *Gold rush in California.*
- I **talk about** people and professions in the past.
- I **find out about** American and UK culture.
- I **act out** buying things in a newsagent's, in a role play.
- I **read about** music and write a project.

Lesson 1

1 Listen and say.

Hi, everyone. My name's Lisa. I'm from the USA. In my country, there are many people with different professions. Can you guess what I want to be? Can you name any other professions?

 musician
 scientist
 inventor

 politician
 builder
 TV presenter
 film star

 journalist
 basketball player
 chef

2 Listen and find out. What does Lisa want to be? Now ask and talk about you.

- Do you want to be a politician?
- Yes, I do. It's my dream!
- I'm not sure. Maybe.
- No, I definitely don't.

3   Listen and do the vocabulary quiz.

This person reads the news and presents programmes on TV. Who is it?

34  Find out the profession of someone who makes bread and cakes.

Lesson 2

4 Listen and read.

 Hi, everyone! Here's an e-zine about famous people in the USA. What are their professions? Who do you admire? POST ✓

Selena Gomez

Selena Gomez is a singer, an actor and a fashion designer. She can also play the guitar, the piano and the drums. Selena Gomez was born in Texas, in the USA. She is bilingual in English and Spanish. Selena loves animals and she's got six dogs from a dog rescue home.

Kobe Bryant

Kobe Bryant is a professional basketball player. He plays for the Los Angeles Lakers and for the national US team. Kobe Bryant is 1.98 metres tall. He has got thousands of fans all over the world. As a very young child, he was brilliant at sport.

 READING TIP Scan the text to find key information.

Mark Zuckerberg

Mark Zuckerberg is the co-inventor of Facebook, a social media website with more than 500 million daily users. At school, he was good at history and languages. Today he is a rich businessman.

Michelle Obama

Michelle Obama is a lawyer. She is the wife of the American politician and first black president of the USA, Barack Obama. Michelle Obama is famous for promoting healthy eating in children.

5 Answer the questions.
1. Who's got thousands of fans?
2. Who can play the drums?
3. Who promotes healthy eating?
4. Who's a rich businessman?

6 Play *Who is it?*

THINKING SKILLS Associating

 She's a singer.

 It's Selena Gomez!

7 Choose and say.
I admire Kobe Bryant because he's a brilliant basketball player!

 Find out one more fact about each person in the text.

Lesson 3

8 Listen to and read the story.

Hi there! People often say the USA is the land of opportunity. The Gold Rush in California was an extraordinary time in American history. This is a historical story about one family.

POST ✓

Gold Rush in California

- What was Amy's father's dream?
- What was Amy's brilliant idea?

1 In 1848, James Marshall was a builder in California. One day when he was at work …

Hey, look! What's this?

It's yellow and shiny. It's gold.

2 Soon the discovery of gold was in the newspapers everywhere in the USA. Amy and her family were in Ohio. Amy's father was a poor farmer. He was very excited.

Let's go to California. We can be rich.

Oh no! I don't think it's a good idea.

But look! It says here that it's easy to find gold.

3 The journey to California in a wagon was long and difficult. At times, it was very cold. At night there were robbers and it was dangerous. Amy and her mother were worried. Amy's father was very happy.

I can't wait to find gold.

I don't believe there's gold for everyone.

Oh dear. I'm sure you're right, Mum.

4 After many weeks, Amy and her family were near the famous hills and rivers of gold in California. There were thousands of miners from all over the world. Many miners were wild and violent.

Ha, ha! Look at this gold. It was in the river this morning.

Hey! You leave that alone. That's my gold.

9 Read and say *True* or *False*. Correct the false sentences.

1 Amy's father was a poor builder in Ohio.
2 The journey to California was short and easy.
3 There were miners from all over the world.
4 Amy's father was in the hills for several days.
5 Amy's mother was a baker at the mining camp.
6 There was lots of gold in Amy's father's bag.

Tiger Time Values — Think about it!

Is it a good idea to depend on luck?

What can you do so that you don't depend on luck?

36

5 Amy's father was excited about his dream of gold. He was in the hills looking for gold with other men for several months.

6 Amy and her mother were scared and worried. At first they were very poor. But one day Amy was very excited.

7 So while Amy's father was away, Amy's mother was a baker at the mining camp and Amy was her helper. Amy's mother's cakes and pies were delicious and very popular.

8 At last Amy's father was back from the hills. He was unhappy and disappointed. After all the months of hard work, there was only a little gold in his bag.

9 You don't need to look for gold any more, thanks to Amy's brilliant idea. There was more gold from baking cakes and pies!

Do you know…?
There were 300,000 gold-seekers in California, from the USA, Europe, Latin America, Australia and China. Some early gold-seekers were very rich, but many gold-seekers were never lucky.

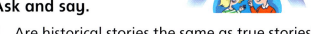

10 Ask and say.

1. Are historical stories the same as true stories?
2. Do you like historical stories? Why? / Why not?
3. What's your favourite part of the story?
4. What's your opinion of Amy, her mother and her father?

Everyday phrases: learn and use!

I don't think it's a good idea.

That's a brilliant idea!

Here you are.

You're back!

GRAMMAR TRACKS

Lesson 4

11 Listen and read. Say who was lucky in the Gold Rush.

Lucky or unlucky?

Jim and Kate **were** from Australia. Before the Gold Rush, they **were** poor but they **were** happy. Jim **was** a builder and Kate **was** a cleaner. Jim and Kate **were** in California from 1851 to 1853. It **wasn't** easy. After the Gold Rush, they **were** still poor. They **weren't** lucky.

Sarah and Tom **were** from Ireland. Before the Gold Rush, they **were** poor and unhappy. Tom **was** a carpenter and Sarah **was** a cook. Tom and Sarah **were** in California in 1849. It **was** very exciting. After the gold rush, they **were** rich and happy. They **were** very lucky.

12 Play *Read every word!*

13 Listen, repeat and learn. Past tense of 'be'

I / He / She It	was	poor. easy.
We / They	were	farmers.

I / He / She It	wasn't	poor. easy.
We / They	weren't	farmers.

Was he / she	a teacher?		he / she was.		he / she wasn't.
Was it	exciting?	Yes,	it was.	No,	it wasn't.
			I was.		I wasn't.
Were you / they	lucky?		we / they were.		we / they weren't.

14 Be a grammar detective!
Look at page 37 in the AB.

When do we use 'was' and 'were'?
What is the short form of 'was not' and 'were not'?

Can you find two examples of 'was' and 'were' in the story?

FAST TRACK GRAMMAR Write five sentences using 'was' and 'were'.

Lesson 5

15 Listen and count the syllables. Say the odd one out.

1. actor   cleaner   inventor   builder
2. scientist   politician   journalist   musician
3. lucky   happy   poor   easy
4. exciting   dangerous   unlucky   disappointed

16 Listen and answer the questions.

When I was little …

	Character	Favourite food	Favourite toy
Jessica	happy, easy to please	spaghetti	red bike
Adam	noisy, naughty	bananas	yellow car
Laura	quiet, shy	chicken	blue bike
Ryan	happy, noisy	spaghetti	red car
Nicholas	shy, easy to please	bananas	yellow bike
Tina	quiet, naughty	chicken	blue car

17 Play *When you were little …*

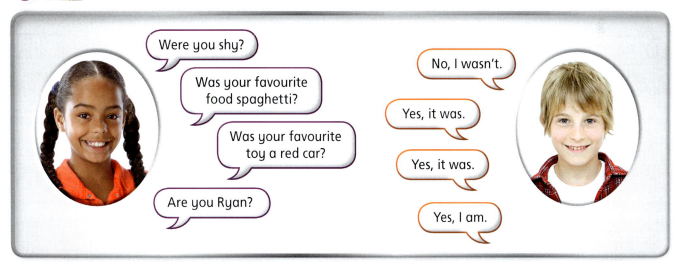

Were you shy?
Was your favourite food spaghetti?
Was your favourite toy a red car?
Are you Ryan?

No, I wasn't.
Yes, it was.
Yes, it was.
Yes, I am.

18 Ask your friends.

Were you shy when you were little?   No, I wasn't.   What was your favourite food?   It was cereal.

FAST TRACK GRAMMAR   Write five sentences about when you were little.

POST ✓

The United States dollar is a world-famous currency. Here are some cool facts about the dollar. Which ones do you think are interesting or surprising?

Lesson 6

19 Listen and read.

The United States dollar

The United States dollar is the official currency of the USA. The sign for the US dollar is $ and the short form is USD. There are one hundred cents to one dollar. There are coins for cents, and banknotes, or bills, for dollars.

Each dollar banknote has got the portrait of a famous US president or politician on it. For example, George Washington is on the one-dollar banknote. He was the first president of the USA.

US dollar banknotes are made of cotton, not paper. They are all the same size. In the past, they were all green. Today you can see different colours on dollar banknotes, such as light purple and yellow. If you look carefully, you can also see a watermark, and tiny red, blue and silver threads. This is to stop people making copies of banknotes.

What do you know about the money in your country?

20 Read and guess. Listen and say the answers.

POST ✓

Here is a fun quiz about the USA! How many questions can you do?

Culture quiz time: The USA

1. What's the capital of the USA?   a) New York   b) Washington D.C.   c) Los Angeles
2. What's the population of the USA?   a) more than 100 million   b) more than 200 million   c) more than 300 million
3. How many states are there in the USA?   a) 48   b) 50   c) 52
4. What's the popular name for the US flag?   a) stars and stripes   b) lines and stars   c) lines and stripes
5. When was the Declaration of Independence?   a) 1721   b) 1754   c) 1776
6. What was George Washington's favourite food?   a) cake   b) ice cream   c) biscuits

In the UK we use pounds and pence. We often say 'p' for pence.

POST ✓

Lesson 7

21 **Listen and read. Say *True* or *False*.**

1. The official name of the UK currency is the British pound.
2. There is a portrait of Queen Elizabeth II on all banknotes.
3. There is a picture of a famous historical building on all banknotes.
4. There are coins for one pound, two pounds and five pounds.
5. In informal English, or slang, people sometimes call a pound a 'quid'.
6. All the banknotes are the same size and colour.

Everyday chit-chat

 How to buy things in a newsagent's

22 **Listen and repeat.**

1. magazine   2. comic   3. packet of mints   4. purse

23 **Listen and read. Repeat.**

Woman: Hello. Do you want to buy the magazine?
Rosa: Oh, yes please. It's for my mum. And I'd like this comic and a packet of mints as well, please. How much is it altogether?
Woman: Well, that's four pounds seventy for the magazine, one pound ninety for the comic and 60p for the mints. So that's seven pounds and twenty pence altogether.
Rosa: Here's seven pounds. Let me look in my purse to see if I've got some small change.
Woman: Thank you. Have you got 20p?
Rosa: Oh dear. No, sorry, I haven't. But here's 50p.
Woman: Don't worry. That's fine. And here's 30p change. Do you need a bag?
Rosa: No, thank you. I can put them in my rucksack. Oops! No, I can't. My rucksack is full.
Woman: OK. Here's a bag.
Rosa: Thank you. Goodbye.

24   **Do a role play.**

Music

Lesson 8

 Listen and read.

Hi there! Here's a cool website about different kinds of American music. Which music do you know? Which do you like?

American music

Many kinds of music were originally from the USA. They still have a big influence on popular music in many countries today.

Jazz music
Jazz music was originally music from a mix of African and American culture. It was first popular in New Orleans at the beginning of the 20th Century. Ella Fitzgerald and Louis Armstrong were famous jazz singers. There were also famous jazz bands such as the New Orleans Rhythm Kings.

Country and western
'Country' music was originally from popular folk songs. 'Western' music was originally from cowboys. Country and western music is a mix of both types of music. It was first popular in the 1920s. The songs often tell stories about people's lives and feelings. Johnny Cash and Glen Campbell were famous country and western singers.

Rap music
Rap music was first popular in New York in the 1970s. The name 'rap' was a slang word for conversation. Rap music is a poem or chant to music with a strong beat. Rap music is an important part of the hip-hop culture of young people in big cities. Hip-hop is also the name of a modern kind of dancing. Jay-Z and Nicki Minaj are two famous rappers.

Rock 'n' roll

Rock 'n' roll was originally from African rhythm and blues music. It was first popular in the 1950s. Bill Haley and the Comets were the first band to have a big hit with the song 'Rock around the clock'. Elvis Presley was a famous rock 'n' roll singer. Rock 'n' roll is also the name of a kind of dancing.

26 Answer the questions.
1. Where was jazz music first popular?
2. Where was 'western' music originally from?
3. What was the name of a big rock 'n' roll hit?
4. What was the name 'rap' from?
5. What's the name of a modern culture and kind of dancing?

27 Listen and identify the music.

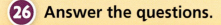

THINKING SKILLS
Associating

 I think it's rap music.

 I agree.

28 Think and say.
Does American music have an influence on popular music in your country?
What kind of music do you like – rap, dance, pop, Latin?

My words to remember
jazz music   country and western   rock 'n' roll   rap music   hip-hop   hit

 Find out the name of a famous jazz band in the USA today.

Project: Quiz on famous people in history

29 **Listen and read.**

Look at my quiz on famous people in history. Do you know the answers? Try not to cheat! (You can check at the bottom of the page.) POST ✓

My quiz on famous people in history

1. Who was George Washington?
2. Were the Wright brothers the inventors of the car?
3. Was Elvis Presley a famous jazz singer?
4. Who was the first person to walk on the moon?
5. Was William Shakespeare a writer?
6. Who were the New Orleans Rhythm Kings?
7. Who was Christopher Columbus?
8. Who were Greta Garbo and Marilyn Monroe?

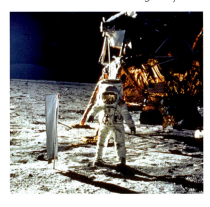

By Duncan

30 **Plan your project.**

1. Think of some famous people in history.
2. Find out about the people.
3. Make notes on your questions and answers.
4. Prepare and write your project.

You can present your project in this way.

Here's the first question in my quiz. Are you ready? Who was George Washington?

➡ AB page 42

Do the Unit 4 Review and self-assessment (Activity Book page 42). Complete your *Progress Journal* for Unit 4.

(1 He was the first president of the USA. 2 No, they weren't. They were the inventors of the aeroplane. 3 No, he wasn't. He was a famous rock 'n' roll singer. 4 The first person to walk on the moon was Neil Armstrong. 5 Yes, he was. William Shakespeare was a writer. 6 They were a famous American jazz band. 7 He was a famous explorer. 8 They were famous American film stars.)

43

5 Past times

In this unit:

- I **name** and **talk about** everyday activities.
- I **listen to** and **read** a legend *Robert the Bruce and the spider*.
- I **ask** and **answer** questions about past events.
- I **find out about** Scottish and UK culture.
- I **act out** telling a friend about something that happened, in a role play.
- I **read about** life in a medieval castle and write a project.

Lesson 1

1 Listen and say.

Tiger Tracks SLN POST ✓

Hello there. I'm Duncan and I'm from Scotland. Here are some typical everyday activities. Can you guess the sentences that are true for me? Which sentences are true for you? What else do you do every day?

1. I **help** at home.
2. I **walk** to school.
3. I **visit** my grandparents.

4. I **watch** TV.
5. I **look after** my pet.
6. I **talk** to my friends.
7. I **use** a computer.

8. I **listen to** music.
9. I **work** hard at school.
10. I **share** things with my friends.

2 Listen and find out. What does Duncan do every day?  Now ask and talk about you.

- Do you help at home?
- Yes, I usually do.
- Yes, I sometimes do.
- No, I never do.

3   Listen and do the vocabulary quiz. Say the verbs.

I go to school by car, but I **** to the park and the shops.

 INTERNET TRACKS Find out the population of Scotland.

Lesson 2

4 Listen and read.

Hi again, everyone! Scotland is a wonderful country. I live in the capital city, Edinburgh, and I love photography. Here's my photo wall with some recent photos of fun places to visit in Edinburgh!

POST ✓

My photo wall

READING TIP: Skim the text to find out what Duncan thinks of each place.

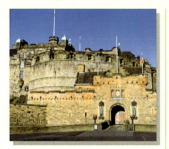

This is Edinburgh Castle. It's a famous medieval castle on top of a high rock. Mary, Queen of Scots lived here many years ago. I visited Edinburgh castle with some friends last weekend. When you're at the castle, there's an amazing view over the city.

Edinburgh Zoo is the most famous zoo in Scotland. There are more than 1,000 different animals. It is also the only zoo in the UK with koalas and giant pandas. Edinburgh Zoo has got beautiful gardens. I love it! It's really cool!

The main shopping street in Edinburgh is Princes Street. It's a very long street with many clothes shops. I shopped there with my mum and dad last Saturday. It was quite boring but I enjoyed taking photos! Afterwards, we walked to Princes Street Gardens and played ball on the grass. It was good fun.

A brilliant place to visit in Edinburgh is the Royal Yacht Britannia. This was the boat of the British Royal family for 40 years. These days the boat is an interesting museum. You can visit the royal bedrooms, living rooms and kitchens. You can also see an old Rolls-Royce car in the garage! It's fantastic!

5 Answer the questions.
1. What is the name of the main shopping street?
2. Where can you see koalas and giant pandas?
3. Where do you get an amazing view of the city?
4. What can you visit on the Royal Yacht Britannia?

6 Play *Find a partner!*

 Let's go to Edinburgh Castle!

 No, I don't want to.

 Good idea! We're partners.

THINKING SKILLS Analysing

7 Choose and say.

I want to visit the Royal Yacht Britannia because I like boats.

INTERNET TRACKS Find out the name of another museum to visit in Edinburgh.

45

Lesson 3

8 Listen to and read the story.

Hi there! This is a famous Scottish legend. It's about how a spider helped Scotland to become independent from England. It's cool what you can learn about life from a little bug! ☺

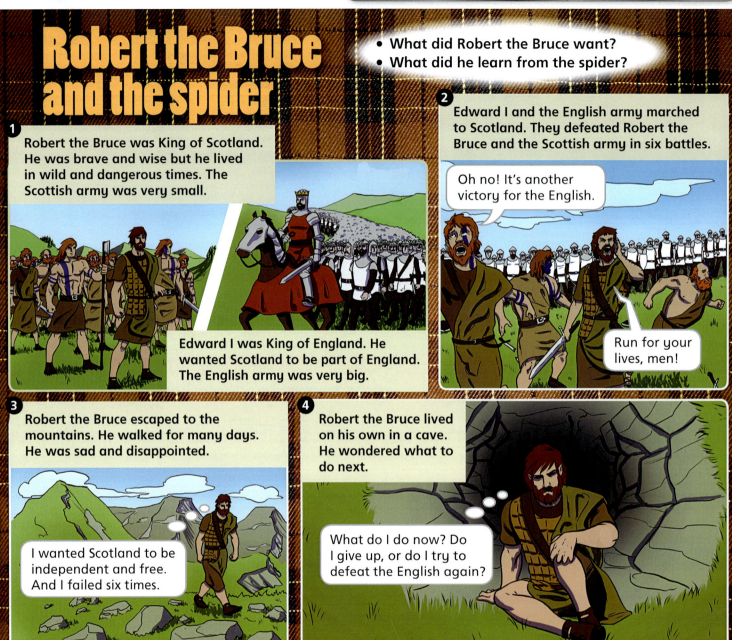

9 Answer the questions.

1. What did Edward I, King of England, want?
2. How many times did he defeat Robert the Bruce?
3. Where did Robert the Bruce escape to?
4. What did Robert the Bruce notice in the cave?
5. How many times did the spider fail to make its web?
6. What did the spider inspire Robert the Bruce to do?

Is it important to try to do things that are difficult?

What do you do when things are difficult?

5 Suddenly Robert noticed a spider on the wall of the cave. He watched the spider as it worked slowly to make its web. The spider climbed up the wall of the cave six times. And six times, it dropped down again.

6 But the spider continued. Robert the Bruce watched as the spider started to make its web for the seventh time.

7 The little spider started spinning its web. Robert the Bruce jumped up and laughed. He was happy and excited.

8 The little spider inspired Robert the Bruce. He formed an army of 5,000 men. In the seventh battle, Robert the Bruce defeated Edward II (Edward I's son) and an enormous English army of 20,000 men.

9 Edward II and his army returned to England. Robert the Bruce was King of Scotland again.

Do you know...?
This legend is the story behind a well-known proverb:
'If at first you don't succeed, try, try, try again.'

10 Ask and say.
1. Do you like reading legends?
2. Many legends have a moral. What's the moral of this legend?
3. What's your favourite part of the story?
4. What's your opinion of Robert the Bruce?

Everyday phrases: learn and use!

What do I do now?

This is incredible!

We're the winners!

Hurray!

47

GRAMMAR TRACKS

Lesson 4

11 Listen and read. Say where Duncan went and what he wanted to see.

Dear Granny and Grandad,
I hope you're well. Last Saturday I **went** to Loch Ness with some of my school friends. We **wanted** to see the famous monster, Nessie! We **walked** along a path by the lake. We **had** a picnic and **stayed** all afternoon. We **talked** and **played** games. It was really good fun. We **listened** and **looked** for Nessie but we **didn't notice** anything strange in the lake :-(. Later we **visited** the Loch Ness museum and **watched** a film about Nessie. We **didn't believe** a lot of the stories about Nessie but we **laughed** a lot and **had** a really great time.
Did you **have** a good weekend? I hope so!
Lots of love,
Duncan

12   Play *Past tense verb tennis!*

13 Listen, repeat and learn.

Past simple tense

I / You / He / She / It / We / They	talk**ed**.
	went to the lake.
	had a good time.

I / You / He / She / It / We / They	**didn't**	talk.
		go to the lake.
		have a good time.

| Did | I / you / he / she / it / we / they | talk? go to the lake? have a good time? | Yes, | I / you / he / she / it / we / they | did. | No, | I / you / he / she / it / we / they | didn't. |

14 Be a grammar detective!
Look at page 47 in the AB.

When do we use the past simple tense?

How do we make the past simple tense of regular verbs?

Which two verbs in the table are irregular?
(You need to learn these!)

Can you find five examples of past simple tense regular verbs in the story?

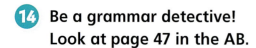 Write five sentences using past simple tense regular verbs.

Lesson 5

15 Listen and count the syllables. Match the sentences with the same number of syllables.

1 I walked along the path.
2 I helped my mum.
3 I visited the castle.
4 I started to laugh.
5 I used my mum's new computer.

a I watched TV.
b I looked after my sister.
c I wanted to see the monster.
d I listened to music.
e I played with my friends.

16 Listen and find out what Duncan did yesterday. Ask a friend.

1 Did you listen to music?
2 Did you walk to school?
3 Did you watch TV?
4 Did you clean your teeth?
5 Did you have homework?
6 Did you visit a friend?
7 Did you go to a supermarket?
8 Did you help at home?

17 Play *Yes, I did!*

Did you laugh yesterday?

Did you use a computer yesterday?

Yes, I did.

Yes, I did.

18 Talk with a friend. Say ten things you didn't do yesterday.

I didn't play football.

I didn't go to the cinema.

 FAST TRACK GRAMMAR Write six sentences about what you did and didn't do yesterday.

Hey, guys! As I'm from Scotland and I'm a boy, Lisa from the USA wants to know if I wear a kilt! The answer is 'no'! But read on and find out more about this Scottish tradition! When do some men wear kilts these days?

POST ✓

Lesson 6

19 Listen and read.

Kilts and tartans

In Scotland there are many cultural traditions.

The tradition of wearing kilts started in the Scottish highlands. A kilt was a piece of cloth. Men tied the kilt round their waists with a belt. They used a sporran, a small leather bag, to keep money and other valuable things in. At night they used the kilt as a blanket. By the 18th century, kilts were like the one in the photo.

The traditional cloth for kilts is tartan. Tartans can be many different combinations of colours. Scottish clans or big family groups traditionally have their own tartan.

Today some men still wear kilts and sporrans for special occasions. These include weddings, parades and Scottish dances where people play traditional music with the famous Scottish bagpipes.

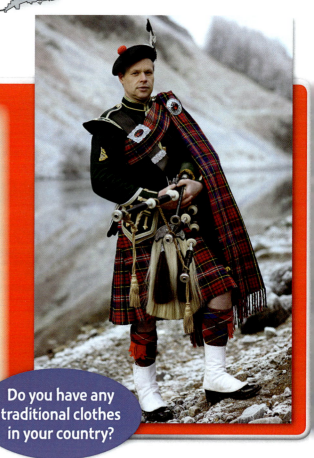

Do you have any traditional clothes in your country?

20 Read and guess. Listen and say the answers.

It's my turn to give you a quiz about Scotland! You already know the answer to number 1! ;-) How many other questions can you answer?

POST ✓

Culture quiz time: Scotland

1. What's the capital of Scotland? a) Glasgow b) Aberdeen c) Edinburgh
2. What's the official language of Scotland? a) Scottish Gaelic b) English c) Scots
3. What's the name of a famous Scottish biscuit? a) ginger biscuit b) cracker c) shortbread
4. Who was Robert Burns? a) a famous king of Scotland b) a famous poet and songwriter c) a famous football player
5. How many islands are part of Scotland? a) more than 390 b) more than 590 c) more than 790
6. What's the famous Scottish food 'haggis' made from? a) meat b) fish c) cheese

In England we haven't got a traditional costume like the Scottish kilt. But at the Tower of London there are famous guards who wear amazing uniforms!

POST ✓

Lesson 7

21 **Listen and read. Say *True* or *False*.**

1. The guards at the Tower of London are called beefeaters.
2. King Henry VIII started the beefeaters in 1485.
3. The beefeaters looked after prisoners and guarded the Crown Jewels.
4. Today the beefeaters guard the Tower and are a popular tourist attraction.
5. There are twenty beefeaters at any one time.
6. It is only men who can be beefeaters.

Everyday chit-chat

 How to tell a friend about something that happened

22 **Listen and repeat.**

1 neighbour   2 puppy   3 collar   4 lead

23 **Listen and read. Repeat.**

Rosa: Guess what happened to me yesterday?
Ollie: What? Go on, tell me!
Rosa: Well, I was at the bus stop after school with my rucksack and books, and our neighbour walked by with a dog.
Ollie: Did you say hello?
Rosa: Yes, I did. She explained that she had a new dog!
Ollie: What kind was it?
Rosa: It was a sweet little puppy – a white Scottish terrier with a tartan collar and lead. Its name's Scottie. Look! Here's a photo!
Ollie: Ahhh. How cute!
Rosa: Yes, I know. But look what happened to my maths book!
Ollie: Oh no, Rosa!

24   **Do a role play.**

CLIL
History

Hi there! Scotland is famous for its medieval castles. Do you think life in a castle in medieval times was easy or difficult? Read on and find out! Enjoy! ☺

POST ✓

Lesson 8

25 Listen and read.

Life in a medieval castle

Medieval castles were homes and fortresses. Castles were often on the top of hills or rocks. This helped to see enemies.

Parts of the castle
Many castles had thick walls, small windows and high towers. They also had dungeons to keep prisoners in. Many castles had a moat of water. People used a drawbridge to cross the moat. They entered the castle through a big gate.

People in the castle
Many different people lived in the castle. These included the lord and lady of the castle, and their family. Knights, cooks, servants and guards also lived in the castle. Sometimes musicians and acrobats visited the castle and performed shows. Many animals, such as dogs and chickens, lived in the castle, too. The castle was a busy and noisy place.

Daily life in the castle
Inside the castle, there was a fire in every room but it was always dark and cold. The servants prepared food in the kitchen and served it on tables in the Great Hall. The lord of the castle often shared a room with his family. People didn't wash often and they usually dropped rubbish in the moat. For this reason, the castle was also smelly and dirty.

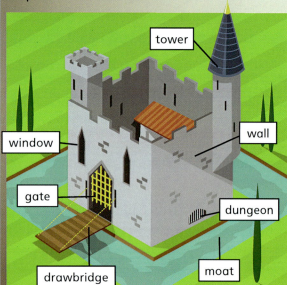

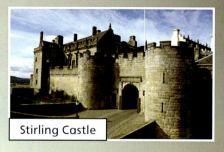

Stirling Castle

Doune Castle

26 Read and correct the sentences.

1. Castles were often near hills or rocks.
2. Many castles had thin walls and big windows.
3. People used a boat to cross the moat.
4. Sometimes the lord and lady performed shows.
5. People usually collected their rubbish.

27 Play *Content chain!*

Castles had dungeons! ...

Castles had dungeons. It was cold! ...

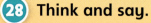

THINKING SKILLS
Critical thinking

28 Think and say.
Are there any medieval castles in your country?
What was it like to live in a medieval castle?
Is life easier or more difficult today?

My world

My words to remember
castle   dungeon   moat
drawbridge   tower   gate

INTERNET TRACKS   Find out the name of a medieval castle in England.

Project: My great-grandparents

29 Listen and read.

Look at my project about my great-grandparents. It's amazing the differences between life in the past and life today! Did my great-grandparents have a car? Did they have a television?

POST ✓

My great-grandparents

When they were young, my great-grandparents lived in a small house in a village in the countryside. My great-grandfather worked in the local post office and my great-grandmother stayed at home. She looked after the children.

They didn't have a car. They walked or cycled everywhere.

They didn't go to a supermarket. They went to a small shop in the village.

They didn't have a washing machine. My great-grandmother washed clothes by hand.

They didn't have a computer or the internet but they enjoyed writing letters and reading books and newspapers.

They didn't have a mobile phone but they had a telephone in the house.

They didn't play computer games but they played card games.

Every week my great-grandmother played the piano and my great-grandfather played cricket at the local village club. My granny says that my great-grandparents were happy but that life is easier today!

By Rosa

30 Plan your project.

1. Prepare questions to ask about your great-grandparents.
2. Interview your parents or grandparents.
3. Make notes about what they say.
4. Prepare and write your project.

You can present your project in this way.

My project is about life in the times of my great-grandparents.

➡ AB page 52

Do the Unit 5 Review and self-assessment (Activity Book page 52). Complete your *Progress Journal* for Unit 5.

53

6 Fruit and vegetables

AIMS

In this unit:

- I **name** and **describe** fruit and vegetables.
- I **listen to** and **read** an adventure story *The jetboat and the crocodile*.
- I **ask** and **answer** questions about fruit and vegetables.
- I **find out about** South African and UK culture.
- I **act out** shopping for food in a market, in a role play.
- I **read about** nutrients in fruit and vegetables and write a project.

Lesson 1

1 Listen and say.

Tiger Tracks SLN POST ✓

 Hi, everyone. My name's Joseph and I'm from South Africa. In my country we've got many different kinds of fruit and vegetables. How many other kinds of fruit and vegetables can you name?

1 pineapple   2 cherries   3 plums

4 raspberries   5 grapes   6 avocado   7 spinach

8 aubergine   9 red pepper   10 cauliflower

2 Listen and find out. Which fruit and vegetables does Joseph like? Now ask and talk about you.

- Do you like pineapple?
- Yes, I love it!
- I quite like it.
- No, I don't like it at all.

3 Listen and do the vocabulary quiz.

They're small, round and sweet. They're green, red or purple. What are they?

54 **INTERNET TRACKS** Find out the name of one more fruit or vegetable that grows in South Africa.

Lesson 2

4 **Listen and read.**

 Hello again! South Africa is in the southern hemisphere and the seasons are different. When is spring, summer, autumn and winter in South Africa? Which fruit and vegetables grow in each season? Read this cool web page and find out! ☺

POST ✓

What's in season in South Africa?

In South Africa there are some delicious fruit and vegetables in every season.

READING TIP: Predict the answers to Joseph's questions before you read.

Spring

Spring is in September, October and November. There are many colourful wild flowers. This is the time of year when oranges, lemons, raspberries and strawberries are in season. Spring is also the time of year for vegetables such as aubergines, cauliflower and spinach.

Summer

Summer is from December until February. It is very hot and there can be short thunderstorms in the afternoon. In summer, cherries, plums, pineapples and grapes are in season. Summer is also the time of year for vegetables such as lettuce and peas.

Autumn

Autumn is in March, April and May. It's warm and it doesn't rain a lot. In autumn, fruit such as apples and avocados are in season. Autumn is also the time of year for vegetables such as mushrooms and peppers.

Winter

Winter is from June to August. It's cold and you need warm clothes. Fruit such as bananas and pears are in season. Winter is also the time of year for vegetables such as carrots and potatoes. The South African vegetable 'waterblommetjie' or 'little water flowers' are also in season in winter. People eat them with meat and potatoes.

In South Africa there aren't any seasons when you can't enjoy delicious fresh fruit and vegetables!

5 Answer the questions.
1. When is summer in South Africa?
2. Which fruit and vegetables grow in spring?
3. When do carrots and potatoes grow?
4. Which fruit and vegetables grow in autumn?
5. When are 'little water flowers' in season?

6 Play *Say the season!*

THINKING SKILLS Classifying

- Bananas!
- They grow in winter. Oranges!
- They grow in spring.

7 Choose and say.

I want to visit South Africa in January when it's summer.

 Find out when peaches are in season in South Africa.

Lesson 3

8 Listen to and read the story.

Hi there! This is an adventure story about four friends on a school trip to Victoria Falls in southern Africa. I love adventure stories! I hope you do, too! ☺ POST ✓

The jetboat and the crocodile

- Where does the jetboat stop?
- What do the children throw at the crocodile?

1 Mosa, Abri, John and Baruti are on a school trip to Victoria Falls.

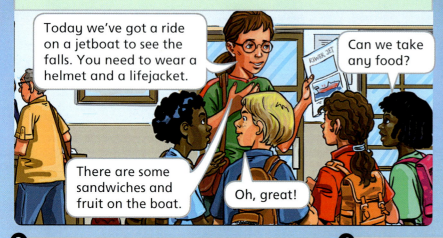

Today we've got a ride on a jetboat to see the falls. You need to wear a helmet and a lifejacket.

Can we take any food?

There are some sandwiches and fruit on the boat.

Oh, great!

2 The children get into the jetboat. At first they go slowly down the river towards Victoria Falls.

Wow! This is amazing.

The scenery is spectacular.

It's fantastic!

And look up there! You can see the famous Victoria Falls Bridge.

3 Suddenly the jetboat's engine makes a loud noise and goes faster. It speeds up the rapids towards the waterfall.

How exciting!

This is scary!

It's very windy.

We're wet.

And we're very close to the rocks.

4 Suddenly the jetboat stops on a rock. The engine is broken.

Oh no! Look! There's a crocodile.

Oh, help! It's hungry.

I know! There are some cheese and chicken sandwiches here.

And there are some plums and grapes.

Quick! Let's throw them at the crocodile.

9 Answer the questions.

1 What do the children need to wear on the trip?
2 Why does the jetboat stop?
3 What do they see in the water?
4 What do they throw at the crocodile?
5 How long do they wait for the helicopter?
6 What do they see from the helicopter?

Is it important to keep safe from wild animals?

How do you keep safe from wild animals?

5 The children throw the sandwiches and fruit at the crocodile. But the crocodile doesn't eat them or go away.

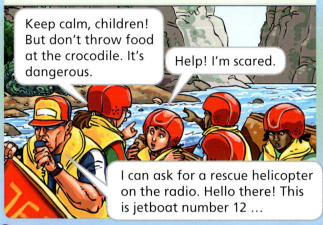

6 The children wait for the helicopter. They're scared. The crocodile is near the boat. Suddenly Abri sees something.

7 Three hours later … the crocodile is still near the boat. It's dark and the helicopter still isn't there.

8 The crocodile swims closer. The children are very scared. Suddenly they hear a noise and look up at the sky.

Do you know…?
The local name for Victoria Falls is 'the smoke that thunders'. You can see the 'smoke' and hear the 'thunder' from 80 kilometres away.

9 Everyone climbs into the helicopter. There is a full moon.

10 Ask and say.

1. Do you like adventure stories? Why? / Why not?
2. What do you think is interesting about Victoria Falls?
3. What do you think is scary about the adventure?
4. Do you want to visit Victoria Falls in a jetboat?

Everyday phrases: learn and use!

How exciting!

This is scary!

Quick!

Keep calm!

GRAMMAR TRACKS

Lesson 4

11 Listen and read. Identify fruit with seeds and fruit with a stone.

Seeds or stone?

There are some small seeds inside grapes. But **there aren't any** small seeds inside cherries. There's a stone.

Are there any small seeds inside strawberries? No, there aren't. But **there are some** small seeds on the outside of strawberries!

There are some small seeds inside raspberries. But **there aren't any** small seeds inside avocados. There's a stone.

12 Play *Seeds or stone?*

Grapes!

Avocados!

There are some small seeds inside grapes.

There aren't any small seeds inside avocados. There's a stone.

13 Listen, repeat and learn.

'a / an', 'some' and 'any'.

There	is a	stone.
	are some	small seeds.

There	isn't a	stone.
	aren't any	small seeds.

Is	there	a	stone?	Yes,	there	is.	No,	there	isn't.
Are		any	small seeds?			are.			aren't.

14 Be a grammar detective! Look at page 57 in the AB.

When do we use 'a' or 'an'?

When do we use 'some'?

When do we use 'any'?

Can you find two examples of 'some' and two examples of 'any' in the story?

58 **FAST TRACK GRAMMAR** Write three sentences using 'some' and three sentences using 'any'.

Lesson 5

15 Listen and count the syllables. Identify the word stress.

1 cherry   apple   pepper   spinach
2 aubergine   banana   tomato   pineapple
3 strawberry   raspberry   carrot   lettuce
4 avocado   cauliflower   helicopter   spectacular

16 Listen and say *True* or *False*. Correct the false sentences.

17 Play *The memory game*.

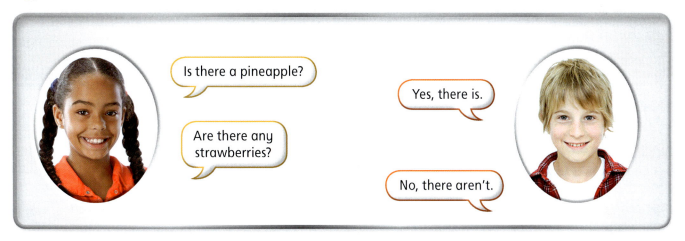

Is there a pineapple?

Yes, there is.

Are there any strawberries?

No, there aren't.

18 Ask and say what's in your classroom.

Is there an interactive whiteboard?

Yes, there is.

Are there any computers?

Yes, there are.

 FAST TRACK GRAMMAR   *Write six questions and answers about what's in your classroom.*

POST ✓

Hello, everyone! In my country there are lots of fruit and vegetable markets. There are also some amazing arts and crafts markets. Read this webpage about arts and crafts markets in South Africa. What do *you* want to look at?

Lesson 6

19 Listen and read.

Arts and crafts markets in South Africa

South Africa is famous for arts and crafts. There are arts and crafts markets in many towns and villages. Arts and crafts markets are lively and colourful. They're fun to visit and you can learn about South African culture.

Arts and crafts markets have lots of different stalls. You can find musical instruments and African masks. You can find pots and baskets. You can also find sculptures and jewellery.

Some things are made from recycled materials such as bottle tops, telephone wire, plastic bags and food labels. For example, there are sculptures made of wire and bottles. There are also brightly coloured 'papier mâché' bowls made from food labels.

In many arts and crafts markets, there are food stalls. You can try traditional South African food. You can also often find jam and sauces made from seasonal fruit and vegetables.

Are there any arts and crafts markets in your country?

20 Read and guess. Listen and say the answers.

POST ✓

Here's a quiz about South Africa! How many questions can you answer?

Culture quiz time: South Africa

1. How many capital cities has South Africa got?   a) one   b) two   c) three
2. What's the population of South Africa?   a) 40 million   b) 50 million   c) 60 million
3. How many official languages are there in South Africa?   a) three   b) five   c) eleven
4. What's South Africa sometimes called?   a) the moonbow nation   b) the rainbow nation   c) the sunshine nation
5. What's the name of a famous mountain in South Africa?   a) Chair Mountain   b) Bed Mountain   c) Table Mountain
6. What's South Africa number one in the world for?   a) plants and flowers   b) fruit and vegetables   c) animals and wildlife

 In the UK there are some arts and crafts markets. We've also got farmers' markets. They're fun to visit and you can buy delicious food!

POST ✓

Lesson 7

21 **Listen and read. Say *True* or *False*.**

1. At farmers' markets people sell fruit, vegetables, meat, cheese and other products.
2. All the products are from the local area.
3. Farmers' markets are usually inside.
4. Farmers' markets usually take place once a week on a different day.
5. The quality of food is not as good as in supermarkets.
6. There are about 500 farmers' markets in the UK.

Everyday chit-chat

! **How to** shop for food in a market

22 **Listen and repeat.**

1. bakery   2. stall   3. pie   4. slice

23 **Listen and read. Repeat.**

Rosa: Mmm, I love the market. This bakery is my favourite stall. The cakes and pies look delicious. Have you got any vegetable pies?
Man: Yes, we have. We've got broccoli-and-cheese pie or spinach pie.
Rosa: Broccoli-and-cheese pie! That sounds delicious. Can I have some, please?
Man: Yes, of course. Do you want a slice or a whole pie?
Rosa: Oh, just a slice, please. That's great. Thanks.
Man: Anything else for you?
Rosa: Oh, yes please. Can I have some of that cake? It looks delicious. What's in it?
Man: Carrots. It's a carrot cake. I cooked it myself.
Rosa: Carrot cake. How amazing! I didn't know you can make a cake with carrots.
Man: Oh, yes. It's very good. Is that everything for you?
Rosa: Yes, thank you.
Man: Right. That's four pounds fifty then, please.

24 **Do a role play.**

61

CLIL
Science

Lesson 8

 25 Listen and read.

 Hi there! South Africa is sometimes called the 'rainbow nation'. But do you know that 'eating a rainbow' of different coloured fruit and vegetables is good for you? Read on to find out more!

POST ✓

Eating a rainbow

Fruit and vegetables contain many essential nutrients that our bodies need.
- Vitamins and minerals keep us healthy, help us grow and can prevent diseases.
- Fibre can prevent hunger and help our digestion.
- Calcium keeps our teeth and bones strong.

Eating fruit and vegetables of different colours is good for your health.

Red fruit and vegetables
These contain vitamins and other nutrients which keep your heart healthy. Examples are cherries, strawberries and red peppers.

Orange and yellow fruit and vegetables
Some orange fruit and vegetables, such as carrots, pumpkins and pineapples, contain Vitamin A and other nutrients which keep your eyes healthy. Citrus fruit, such as oranges and lemons, contain lots of Vitamin C which is important for your general health.

Green fruit and vegetables
These contain fibre, calcium, Vitamin C and other nutrients which keep you healthy and strong. Examples are spinach, lettuce and green grapes.

Blue and purple fruit and vegetables
These contain Vitamin C, fibre and other nutrients which help your body absorb essential minerals. Examples are aubergines, plums and purple grapes.

White fruit and vegetables
These contain nutrients which are good for your heart and stomach. Examples are bananas, cauliflower, mushrooms and potatoes.

It's easy and fun to stay healthy eating fruit and vegetables! Just remember to put a 'rainbow' on your plate!

THINKING SKILLS
Categorising

26 Answer the questions.
1 What do fruit and vegetables contain that our bodies need?
2 What do vitamins and minerals do?
3 What can fibre do?
4 What does calcium do?
5 What colours are in the fruit and vegetable 'rainbow'?

27 **Play *Rainbow chain!***

 Red peppers! ...
Oranges! ...
  Spinach! ...

28 Think and say.
I eat lots of green fruit and vegetables.
I eat some orange and yellow fruit and vegetables.
I don't eat any blue or purple vegetables.

My world

My words to remember
nutrient   vitamin   mineral   calcium   fibre   disease

 Find out the name of one more fruit or vegetable in each colour group.

Project: My food diary

29 **Listen and read.**

 It's interesting to keep a food diary! Read my report. Do I eat a variety of fruit and vegetables? Do I eat five portions every day? POST ✓

My food diary

By Duncan

On Monday I had orange juice and cereal for breakfast. At break, I had some biscuits and a banana. For lunch, I had meat, potatoes and peas. In the afternoon, for a snack I had a sandwich and apple juice. For dinner, I had pizza with mushrooms and red peppers.

On Tuesday I had milk, toast and an apple for breakfast. At break, I had a raspberry yoghurt. For lunch, I had vegetable soup and a burger. In the afternoon, for a snack I had milk and a banana. For dinner, I had chicken and salad.

On Wednesday I had orange juice and toast for breakfast. At break, I had a cheese and tomato sandwich. For lunch, I had fish, potatoes and spinach. In the afternoon, for a snack I had some biscuits and water. For dinner, I had cauliflower cheese and carrots.

30 Plan your project.

1. Think of food you eat every day.
2. Complete your food diary.
3. Find photos or draw pictures to illustrate your diary.
4. Prepare and write your project.

You can present your project in this way.

This is my food diary. Every day I eat lots of different kinds of fruit and vegetables.

➡ AB page 62

Do the Unit 6 Review and self-assessment (Activity Book page 62). Complete your *Progress Journal* for Unit 6.

7 Holiday in the city

In this unit:
- I **name** and **describe** clothes.
- I **listen to** and **read** a photo story *A happy coincidence*.
- I **ask** and **say** what people want.
- I **find out about** places to visit in London.
- I **find out** about where people went and their opinions.
- I **read about** art and write a project.

Lesson 1

1 Listen and say.

Tiger Tracks SLN POST ✓

 Hi, everyone – Rosa here! I'm really excited. Steve, Sita, Lisa, Joseph, Duncan and I are going to London for a holiday! Look at the clothes. Can you guess what I'm taking with me? How many other clothes can you name?

1.  jeans
2.  jacket
3.  fleece
4.  trainers
5.  sandals
6.  dress
7.  cap
8.  cropped trousers
9.  short-sleeved shirt
10.  top

2 Listen and find out. What's Rosa taking on holiday? 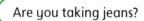 Now ask and talk about you.

- Are you taking jeans?
- Yes, definitely.
- I'm not sure.
- No, I don't think so.

3   Listen and do the vocabulary quiz.

You wear these in summer without socks. What are they?

 64 **INTERNET TRACKS** Find out about the weather in London in July. Is Rosa taking the right clothes?

Lesson 2

4 Listen and read.

 Hello again! Some people say that London is the fashion capital of the world. Read this teen magazine article about fashion in London this summer. Which clothes do you like? Which clothes don't you like?

POST ✓

Look cool – whatever the weather!
Do you want to look cool in London this summer?

READING TIP Look at the photos as you read to check your understanding.

In London in summer the weather is sometimes hot and sunny but it's sometimes cold and rainy. Our models are wearing their favourite clothes for summertime in the city. They show you how to look cool in London whatever the weather!

Gina's wearing a trendy orange dress and sandals. She's also got a light denim jacket to put on if it's cold.

Dave's wearing a short-sleeved, checked shirt and classic blue jeans. He's also wearing popular new-style trainers.

Do you like these clothes? Which are your favourite clothes for summer?

THINKING SKILLS
Observing and memorising

5 Answer the questions.
1 What's the weather like in summer in London?
2 Who's got a light denim jacket?
3 Who's wearing new-style trainers?
4 What kind of dress is Gina wearing?
5 What kind of shirt is Dave wearing?

6 Play *Remember the clothes!*

 I think he's wearing a blue shirt!

I think he's wearing white trainers!

7 Choose and say.

My favourite clothes for this summer are cropped trousers, trainers and a cap.

INTERNET TRACKS Find out the name of a clothes shop for young people in London.

65

Lesson 3

8 Listen to and read the story.

Hi there! This is a photo story about our Tiger Tracks SLN summer trip to London and why we've all got the same T-shirts. I think they're great! Do you agree? POST ✓

A happy coincidence

- What's Lisa's problem?
- What's the coincidence?

1 Lisa, Joseph, Steve and Sita arrive at the hostel from the airport. Rosa and Duncan are there to meet them.

- Hi, everyone!
- Welcome to London!
- Thanks. It's great to be here.
- Yes, it is. But I've got a problem. My luggage wasn't on the plane and I've got no clothes.

2 Later the children talk about what they want to do.

- Hey, guys! What do you want to do?
- I want to go sightseeing.
- Where do you want to go?
- I want to see the famous clock, Big Ben.
- Me too. That's a great idea.

3 But Lisa is feeling miserable. She doesn't want to go sightseeing. She wants her luggage.

- I'm fed up. I want my clothes. I've got T-shirts, cropped trousers and sandals in my luggage and they aren't here.
- Hey, Lisa. I've got an idea. Do you want to go shopping?
- Oh, yes, I do. That's a good idea. Thanks, Rosa.

4 Duncan, Steve, Sita and Joseph go sightseeing. Lisa and Rosa go shopping.

- See you guys later!
- Yes. Enjoy Big Ben!
- Thanks! Goodbye!
- Bye!

9 Answer the questions.

1. What do Sita, Steve and Joseph want to do?
2. What does Lisa want to do?
3. What does Lisa buy?
4. What do Duncan, Sita, Steve and Joseph give Lisa?
5. What do they all wear for a group photo?
6. Why is Lisa happy at the end of the story?

Tiger Time Values — Think about it!

Is it important to be kind to your friends if they're fed up or miserable?

How are you kind to your friends?

66

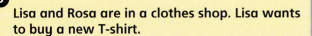

5 Lisa and Rosa are in a clothes shop. Lisa wants to buy a new T-shirt.

6 Duncan, Steve, Sita and Joseph see Big Ben and go for a walk in the streets of London. But they feel sorry for Lisa.

7 Later, all the children meet back at the hostel.

8 Lisa opens the present. She can't believe her eyes.

Do you know...?
Millions of people from all over the world visit London to go sightseeing and shopping. Two big London airports (Heathrow and Gatwick) have more than 100 million passengers each year.

9 Rosa, Duncan, Steve, Sita and Joseph all buy tiger T-shirts. They wear their tiger T-shirts for a group photo in the hostel.

10 Ask and say.
1. Do you like photo stories? Why? / Why not?
2. What's your favourite part of the story?
3. Do you like wearing the same clothes as your friends?
4. What kind of T-shirt do you want?

Everyday phrases: learn and use!

I'm fed up.

It's really cool!

What a shame!

What a coincidence!

GRAMMAR TRACKS

Lesson 4

11 Listen and read. Say what the boy wants and what his friend wants.

- I **want to** buy a shirt, please.
- I **want** a short-sleeved shirt for summer.
- Yes, I **do**. Thank you.
- I **want** blue or green, please.
- No, she **doesn't**. She **wants** a jacket.
- **What** kind of shirt **do** you **want**?
- They're here. **Do** you **want** to try one on?
- **What** colour **do** you **want**?
- **Does** your friend **want** a shirt as well?

12 Act out the dialogue. Ask for different things.

I want to buy some trainers.

What kind of trainers do you want?

13 Listen, repeat and learn.

Present simple review: 'want'

| He / She | wants | a jacket. / to go shopping. |

| He / She | doesn't want | a jacket. / to go shopping. |

| Does | he / she | want | a jacket? / to go shopping? | Yes, he / she does. | No, he / she doesn't. |

14 Be a grammar detective!
Look at page 67 in the AB.

What kind of words do we use after i) 'want' and ii) 'want to'?

When do we add an 's' to 'want'?

What are the short forms of 'do not want' and 'does not want'?

Can you find three examples of 'want' in the story?

 FAST TRACK GRAMMAR Write five sentences using 'want'.

68

Lesson 5

15 **Listen and count the syllables. Identify the sentence stress.**

1. Does she want to go shopping?
2. Does he want a biscuit?
3. Do they want to play football?
4. He wants a glass of water, please.
5. What do you want to do?
6. What do you want?
7. What colour do you want?
8. I want blue, please.

16 **Listen and say who it is.**

17 **Play *Guess the person.***

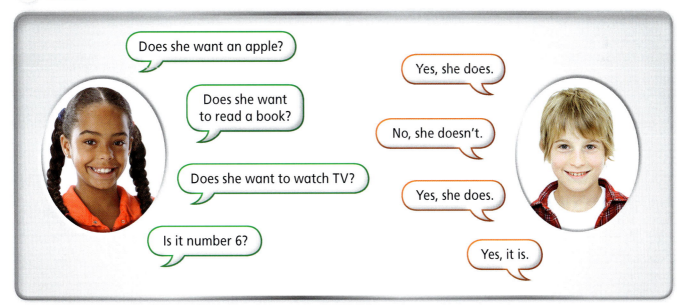

Does she want an apple?
Yes, she does.
Does she want to read a book?
No, she doesn't.
Does she want to watch TV?
Yes, she does.
Is it number 6?
Yes, it is.

18 **Find out what a friend wants. Tell the class.**

Susana wants a glass of water.
David wants to play a computer game.

 FAST TRACK GRAMMAR *Write five sentences about what your friend wants.*

POST ✓

Hello, everyone! Here's a brilliant website we used to decide where to go in London. Can you guess where we went?

Cult

Lesson 6

19 Listen and read.

TOP SIX PLACES TO VISIT IN LONDON

THE LONDON EYE
The London Eye is an enormous wheel. It moves very slowly and takes half an hour to go all the way round. During the trip, you can sit down or stand up and enjoy magnificent views over London.

THE NATIONAL GALLERY
The National Gallery is a world-famous art gallery with lots of amazing paintings. Here you can find works of art by many English and European artists. A famous painting in the National Gallery is 'The Rokeby Venus' by the Spanish painter Diego Velázquez.

MADAME TUSSAUDS
Madame Tussauds is a museum of wax figures. You see famous people from the past and present, including kings, queens, politicians, actors and sports heroes. In the gallery of Hollywood legends and superstars you can stand next to Shrek, Buzz Lightyear or Johnny Depp.

THE NATURAL HISTORY MUSEUM
At the Natural History Museum, there is a fascinating exhibition of dinosaurs with 3D images of how dinosaurs looked and moved. You can also see a life-sized blue whale and a 40-million-year-old spider.

THE SCIENCE MUSEUM
The Science Museum gives you an amazing interactive learning experience. You find out about science over the last 300 years. You learn about the history of machines from the steam engine, to the first car, to early aeroplanes and modern space rockets.

THE PLANETARIUM
At the Planetarium, there are 3D shows that take you on a tour of the universe. You discover planets and galaxies. You learn about the birth of stars and solar storms. You fly into the centre of the sun and 'land' on Mars!

20 Listen and answer. Where did they go on each day?

Monday	Tuesday	Wednesday	Thursday	Friday	Saturday	Sunday

Here's a group photo of us at my aunt's house. Read and find out our opinions of the holiday!

Lesson 7

21 Listen and read. What were their favourite places in London?

My favourite place was the Science Museum. It was really interesting. There were so many things to touch and to play with! I really enjoyed learning about how old steam engines work. I want to go back to the Science Museum again one day!

I didn't have a favourite place. I enjoyed everything! The National Gallery was a big surprise. It was brilliant! There were some beautiful paintings by famous artists. I didn't like art before this holiday, but I do now!

My favourite place was the Natural History Museum. It was awesome. I loved the dinosaurs and the enormous blue whale. I also really enjoyed the planetarium. It was amazing to learn about the stars at night and to 'land' on Mars!

I loved everything on this holiday! It was really cool after my luggage arrived! I liked learning about fossils at the Natural History Museum. I also really enjoyed the wax figures at Madame Tussauds. It was funny to stand near so many famous people in the same room!

Number one for me was the London Eye! It was amazing! We went up very high and had an incredible view over London. I also enjoyed the Natural History Museum. There wasn't time to see everything in the museum but I loved the exhibition of dinosaurs.

My favourite place in London was the park, Kensington Gardens. It was very peaceful and had beautiful trees and flowers. I loved seeing Big Ben. I also enjoyed looking at the shops. There was a great atmosphere in London and I want to go back there again one day.

22 Listen and say *True* or *False*. Correct the false sentences.

23 Say where you want to go in London and why.

I want to go to the Natural History Museum because I'm interested in volcanoes.

71

Art

Lesson 8

 Listen and read.

 Hi there! This article helps you to look at art and talk about paintings. I think it's cool. I hope you enjoy it, too! ☺ POST ✓

Looking at art

Types of paintings
When you visit an art gallery, there are different types of paintings. These include portraits, landscape and still life paintings. Portraits are paintings of individual people. Landscape paintings are views of the countryside. Still life paintings show objects, flowers, fruit or vegetables.

Differences in paintings
Some artists paint with oils. Some artists paint with water colours.

Some paintings are realistic. They show things as they are in real life. Some paintings are abstract. They show combinations of lines, shapes and colours.

Some paintings are full of bright colours and light. Some paintings are dark with tones of black and grey.

Some paintings are very big and cover the wall of a room. Some paintings are very small and you need to look carefully to see the detail.

How to look at paintings
When you look at a painting for the first time, use your eyes to 'go for a walk' around the painting. Look at the top, the bottom, the middle, the things that are close, and the things that are far away. Notice and think about:
- the scene and what's happening.
- the people and what they're feeling or thinking.
- the objects and the colours.
- the mood and the atmosphere.
- how the painting makes you feel.

When you look at a painting like this, it helps you to give a personal response and to think in a critical and creative way.

 Answer the questions.

1. What are portraits?
2. What are landscape paintings?
3. What do still life paintings show?
4. What do realistic paintings show?
5. What do abstract paintings show?

THINKING SKILLS
Critical thinking and creativity

 Think and say.

Do you like looking at paintings?

Do you think it's interesting to learn about art?

Describe and talk about the paintings.

 In this painting, I can see a woman.

There are some flowers.

 I like this painting because it's colourful.

My words to remember
portrait   landscape
oils   still life
water colours
realistic   abstract

  Find out the name of a famous English landscape painter.

Project: A famous painting with people

28 Listen and read.

Here's my project about a famous painting with people. What's the name of the artist? What's the mood of the painting?

POST ✓

The title of this painting is *The Reverend and Mrs Palmer-Lovell and their daughters Georgina and Christina*. It's by Augustus Leopold Egg. He painted it in the nineteenth century.

In this painting the family are in the living room and there are lots of paintings on the wall.

Mrs Palmer-Lovell is wearing a white dress. She's playing the piano. She's feeling calm.

The Reverend Palmer-Lovell is wearing a black suit. He's listening to the music.

There are two children in the picture and there's another woman, too. The woman is wearing a green dress. She's looking after the children. One girl is wearing a green dress. She's dancing. The other girl is wearing a white dress with a blue bow.

This painting makes me feel happy because of the bright colours and the calm mood.

By Duncan

29 Plan your project.

1. Choose a famous painting with people.
2. Make notes to describe the painting.
3. Think about your personal response.
4. Prepare and write your project.

You can present your project in this way.

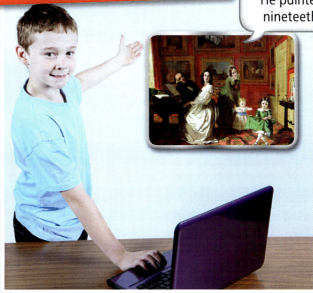

This painting is by Augustus Leopold Egg. He painted it in the nineteenth century.

➡ AB page 72

Do the Unit 7 Review and self-assessment (Activity Book page 72). Complete your *Progress Journal* for Unit 7.

73

Earth Day

1 **Listen and read.**

Hi, everyone! Earth Day is a special day that we often celebrate in the UK. Here's a brilliant website where you can find out all about it. Enjoy! :-) POST ✓

What is Earth Day?

Earth Day facts
On Earth Day we learn about the plants and animals that live on Earth. Some of the oldest living things are trees. In Wales there is a tree that is 5,000 years old. It's the same age as the pyramids in Egypt!

Earth Day activities
Many young people celebrate Earth Day with activities to protect the planet. They plant trees, walk to school, recycle paper and find out about endangered animals. They also think about what they can do to protect the Earth's resources.

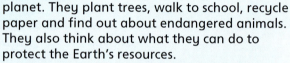

The celebration of Earth Day is nearly fifty years old. It's on 22nd April every year. Earth Day is a day when we remember that life on Earth is very important and we think about how we need to look after our planet and protect it.

What's special about Earth Day?
How do you celebrate Earth Day in your country?

2 **Listen and read.**

Hello again! For our Earth Day party this year we're making chocolate trees. They're a delicious treat! Do you want to make them, too? Here's what you need to do! POST ✓

How to make chocolate trees

You need:
- milk chocolate (250 grams for 4 trees)
- 12 small green sweets (for the leaves)
- wax paper
- baking tray
- small plastic bag
- scissors

What to do
1. Put wax paper on a baking tray.
2. Break the chocolate into small pieces. Put the pieces in a bowl.
3. Melt the chocolate in the microwave and stir it. Be careful! ⚠
4. Put the chocolate in a small plastic bag. Close the bag and cut off the corner.
5. Pipe the chocolate into tree shapes on the wax paper.
6. Add three sweets to each tree for the leaves.
7. Wait until the chocolate is hard. Take the trees off the paper and eat them!

Delicious!

New Year

1 Listen and read.

 Hi there! In Scotland we celebrate New Year. New Year is a very popular festival for Scottish people. You can find out about it here.

New Year in Scotland

For many people in Scotland, the main celebration is New Year's Eve or Hogmanay. One Hogmanay tradition is to clean the house on 31st December. This is to prepare for the New Year. Many people have parties with their families and friends. When the clock strikes twelve at midnight, there are fireworks. People sing and wish each other a happy New Year. Another Hogmanay tradition is 'first footing'. People visit their neighbours' houses after midnight to celebrate.

New Year Traditions

In some parts of Scotland, people stay at home on New Year's Eve. They are waiting for a dark-haired visitor. The visitor brings a piece of coal, some bread, some money and some leaves. These things bring good luck! The coal keeps the house warm. The bread makes sure there is always something to eat. The money makes sure they won't need money and the leaves are for a long life.

Another tradition is to make New Year Resolutions on 1st January. People look back at the year before and decide what they want to do in the New Year. Some people want to learn something new, like a new sport. And some people want to stop doing something – like eating chocolate!

What's special about New Year in Scotland? How do you celebrate New Year in your country?

2 Listen and read. Sing.

Hello again! This is a famous Scottish song we always sing at midnight on New Year's Eve. 'Auld lang syne' means 'Old days long ago'. Why don't you learn the song and sing it with your friends and family on New Year's Eve? It's good fun! I hope you enjoy it! ☺

Auld lang syne

Should old acquaintance be forgot,
And never brought to mind.
Should old acquaintance be forgot,
And auld lang syne.

Chorus
For auld lang syne, my dear,
for auld lang syne,
we'll take a cup of kindness yet,
for auld lang syne.

Carnival

1 Listen and read.

 Hi, everyone. I'm really excited – it's Carnival time! Here's a website which tells you all about Carnival in the USA. It's a lot of fun! POST ✓

Carnival in the USA

People celebrate Carnival or Mardi Gras in many cities in the USA. Mardi Gras is a festival that is originally from Roman times in Italy and France. The French introduced Mardi Gras to the USA in the early 17th Century.

Mardi Gras means 'Fat Tuesday' in French.

The most famous city for Mardi Gras in the USA is New Orleans. There are many colourful parades with floats and music in the streets. There are also many picnics and parties.

Many people wear fancy dress or costumes of purple, green and gold. These are the traditional colours of Mardi Gras. People also often wear long bead necklaces and beautiful eye masks.

During the 'little rascals' parade children ride on floats. And there is even a fancy dress parade for dogs called Barkus!

Many visitors from all over the world come to New Orleans for Mardi Gras. People wear amazing clothes, make new friends and have a fantastic time.

What's interesting or surprising about Mardi Gras in the USA? What do you like about Carnival in your country?

2 Listen and read.

 Hello again! For Mardi Gras this year we're making beautiful eye masks. Do you want to make an eye mask, too? Here's what you need to do. POST ✓

How to make a Mardi Gras eye mask

You need:
- black, white or coloured card
- glitter
- sequins
- glue
- elastic
- scissors
- tape
- small coloured feathers

What to do

1 Draw the shape of an eye mask on the card.
2 Cut out the mask and holes for the eyes.
3 Make tiny holes on the sides of the mask.
4 Attach elastic to fit the mask round your head.
5 Put glue on the mask and add glitter and sequins.
6 Use tape to add feathers to the mask.

Fabulous!

Songs bank

Let's communicate!

Chorus
Life is fantastic!
Technology is great!
We've got gadgets.
Let's communicate!

How about a chat today?
Call me on your mobile phone.
We've got lots to talk about.
I don't want to feel alone.

Chorus

Why not send a message?
Turn on your new webcam.
I can see your smiling face.
Click, click, and here I am!

Chorus

Why not send an email?
Write what you want to say.
Send it from your tablet.
I can answer straight away.

Chorus

The Cool Crowd

Come and join the Cool Crowd, they're playing in the sea.
They're doing sport and having fun, they're happy and they're free.

Hey, hey, a boy is windsurfing, he's riding a big wave.
Water's spraying everywhere, he's trying to be brave.

Hey, hey, a girl is water-skiing, the wind's blowing in her hair.
She's moving very fast and laughing without a care.

Hey, hey, some boys are snorkelling, they're looking at a shell.
They're finding crabs and watching multi-coloured fish as well.

Hey, hey, some girls are kitesurfing, they're holding a red kite.
They're wearing yellow lifejackets, and the sun is shining bright.

Come and join the Cool Crowd, they're playing in the sea.
They're doing sport and having fun, they're happy and they're free.

Red Alert!

Global warming is here.
The Earth is getting hotter.
It's harder for wild animals
To find their food and water.

Chorus
Red alert! Red alert!
Save tigers and rhinos, too!
Red alert! Red alert!
It's up to me and you.

Pollution is a problem.
Rubbish in rivers and seas.
Animals poisoned by chemicals
And dying from disease.

Chorus…
Save elephants and pandas, too!

People cut down forests
Where wild animals roam.
They lose their food and water.
They lose their natural home.

Chorus…
Save gorillas and leopards, too!

People hunting animals
For their skins or horns.
Selling baby animals
Soon after they are born.

Chorus…
Save polar bears and eagles, too!

Who was it?

Who talked to the film star on the radio?
Did you talk to the film star on the radio?
Who me? Oh no! Not me!
I didn't talk to the film star on the radio.
It was Gavin!

Who helped the chef in the burger bar?
Did you help the chef in the burger bar?
Who me? Oh no! Not me!
I didn't help the chef in the burger bar.
It was Maya!

Who watched the inventor on the TV show?
Did you watch the inventor on the TV show?
Who me? Oh no! Not me!
I didn't watch the inventor on the TV show.
It was Lucas!

The fruit and veg song

We eat fruit and vegetables in every season.
They're delicious but it's not the only reason.
Fruit and veg have calcium, minerals and fibre, too.
Fruit and veg have vitamins and they're good for you.

Some fruit and veg are red, some are purple or blue.
Some fruit and veg are orange, some are yellow, too.
Some fruit and veg are green, and some are white.
Fruit and veg keep you healthy, happy and bright.

Fruit and veg grow in the summer, autumn, winter and spring.
You eat them cooked or raw, on their own or with something.
Some fruits have got a stone, some fruits have got seeds
And they have lots of nutrients that your body needs.

We eat fruit and vegetables in every season…

Tiger Time holiday song

Chorus
We're on holiday in London city.
The shops are full and the parks are pretty.
We want to look cool whatever the weather.
We want to have fun and spend time together.

We want to wear shorts, sandals and a top.
We want the sun to shine and the rain to stop.
We want to visit the planetarium and learn about the stars.
We want to discover the universe and 'land' on Mars!

We want to visit a gallery and see amazing art.
We want to learn about dinosaurs right from the start.
We want to see wax figures from the past.
Sports heroes and superstars – what a blast!

We want to travel in a capsule on the London Eye
And get a view of the city from way up high.
We want to go shopping. How about you?
We'd love you to join us and come along, too!

Macmillan Education Limited
4 Crinan Street
London N1 9XW

Companies and representatives throughout the world

ISBN 978-0-230-48376-7
Pack ISBN 978-0-230-48410-8

Text © Carol Read and Mark Ormerod 2015
Additional material by Kerry Powell
Design and illustration © Macmillan Education Limited 2015
The author/s has/have asserted his/her/their rights to be identified
as the author/s of this work in accordance with the Copyright,
Designs and Patents Act 1988.

This edition published 2015
First edition entitled "Tiger Tracks" published 2013 by Macmillan
Education Limited

All rights reserved; no part of this publication may be reproduced,
stored in a retrieval system, transmitted in any form, or by any
means, electronic, mechanical, photocopying, recording, or
otherwise, without the prior written permission of the publishers.

Original design by Blooberry Design Ltd
Page make-up by Andrew Magee Design Ltd
Illustrated by Vladimir Aleksic (Beehive), Humberto Blanco (Sylvie
Poggio), Ted Brandt (Bright Agency), Kevin Hopgood (Beehive),
Ann Kronheimer, Paul McCaffrey (Sylvie Poggio), Andrew Painter,
Andy Parker, Shahab Shamshirsaz (Sylvie Poggio), Emma Shaw
Smith (Sylvie Poggio), Simon Smith (Beehive) and Tony Forbes
(Sylvie Poggio).
Cover design by Astwood Design Consultancy
Cover photographs by Stockbyte/PunchStock, Getty, Thinkstock,
Corbis, DigitalStock/Corbis, Macmillan Publishing Ltd/Stuart Cox
Songs produced and arranged by Tom, Dick and Debbie
Productions
Recordings produced and arranged by RBA Productions
Pictures researched by Victoria Gaunt

Authors' acknowledgements
We would like to thank everyone at Macmillan Education in the
UK and in Spain who has helped us in the development and
the production of these materials. We would also like to thank
all the teachers who have taken time to read, pilot and give
feedback at every stage of writing the course. Special thanks from
Carol to Alan, Jamie and Hannah for their encouragement and
support. Special thanks from Mark to Carlos for his patience and
understanding.

Acknowledgments
The publishers would like to thank the following teachers:
Amparo Fernández Ortiz, CEIP La Patacona, Alboraya, Valencia;
Anna Esteban Nieto, Escola Jaume Ferran I Clua, Valldoreix,
Barcelona; Carlota López Petidier, CEIP Miguel de Cervantes,
Torrejón de Ardoz, Madrid; María del Mar Rodríguez Rodríguez,
Escola Els Pins, Barcelona; Mª Inmaculada Cercadillo Torrecilla,
CEIP Gabriel García Márquez, Getafe, Madrid; Paco Sansaloni
Felis, CEIP Cervantes, Gandía, Valencia; Patricia Meneses Dekker,
Escola Esteve Barrachina, Sitges, Barcelona; Teresa Rofes Bauzá,
Escola Barcelona, Barcelona.

The authors and publishers would like to thank the following for
permission to reproduce their photographs:
Alamy/James Davies p75(tcl), Alamy/DustyDingo p15(bcl),
Alamy/Alan Gallery p7(tr), Alamy/Michael D Griffin p4(9), Alamy/

imagebroker p14(9), Alamy/Blend Images p14(4), Alamy/Pawel
Libera Images p7(cr), Alamy/Radius Images p20(3), Alamy/Justin
Leighton p22(cr), Alamy/lowefoto p7(br), Alamy/mainpicture
p22(tcr) Alamy/louise murray p20(5), Alamy/Ben Nicholson
p10(cm), Alamy/Stuart Pearce p14(2), Alamy/Image Source
Plus p20(1), Alamy/Kumar Sriskandan p14(8), Alamy/ Cre8tive
Studios p79(cl), Alamy/Art Directors & TRIP p64(10), Alamy/Martin
Valigursky p12(cl), Alamy/ Westend61 GmbH p22(cr); **Bananastock**
p29(ml,r); **BrandX** pp24(2), 25(cr); **The Bridgeman Art Library**
pp72(cl,cm,cr), The Bridgeman Art Library/Bonhams London YUK
pp73(cl,bcr); **Comstock Images** p79(cr); **Corbis** pp14(6), 75(tcr),
Corbis/2/Ocean p65(cr), Corbis/Imagesource p14(5), Corbis/
Markus Giolas/LuckyPix p74(cm), Corbis/Robert Michael p20(2),
Corbis/Kennan Harvey/Aurora Open p15(tcr), Corbis/Joe Stevens./
Retna Ltd p35(tl), Corbis/Krista Rossow/National Geographic
Society p76(tcl), Corbis/Klaus Tiedge p39(tr); **Creatas** pp32(cl),
78(cl); **Digital Stock** pp28(a,c), DigitalStock/Corbis p30(cr); **Digital
Vision** p24(4), 32(tcr); **Fitzwilliam museum** p10(bcm); **Getty
Images** pp22(bcr), 24(6), 25(tr), 32(bcr), 79(tl,tr), Getty Images
p21(cr), 35(tr), 74(tcr), 76(tcl),Getty Images/AFP p10(cr), Getty
Images/Nathan Blaney p5(cl), Getty Images/Blend Images p14(1),
Getty Images/Tony Burns p15(bcr), Getty Images/Rex Butcher
p70(br), Getty Images/Reggie Casagrande pp12(tcl), 77(tr), Getty
Images/Photo and Co p14(10), Getty Images/Lucy Davey p5(cr),
Getty Images/Fazer44 p33(tl), Getty Images/altrendo images
p14(3), Getty Images/Brand New Images p75(cr), Getty Images/
Paul Kennedy p15(tcl), Getty Images/Ron Levine p13(cmr), Getty
Images/MonishM p24(7), Getty Images/Stuart Pearce p20(4), Getty
Images/Jeremy Vickers Photography p31(cr), Getty Images/Lonely
Planet p70(tcr), Getty Images/Bobbi Tull p72(cml), Getty Images/
Westend61 p13(cml), Getty Images/WireImage p35(cl); **Image
100** p32(cr); **John Foxx Images** p24(9); **Macmillan Education
Ltd**/Paul Bricknell pp2(bl,br), 8(l,r), 12(bl,br), 18(l,r), 19(l), 22(bl,
br), 28(r,l), 32(br,bl), 38(l, ml), 68(l,r), 72(bl,bm), Macmillan
Education Ltd\David Tolley/Dean Ryan p4(1); **National History
Museum** p70(tcr); **Pathfinder** p29(l); **Photodisc** pp24(1,5,8,10),
25(hippos,flamingos), 28(d), 32(tcl,bcl), 74(tcl), 78(tl,tr); **Photoshot**
p23(cl), Photoshot/NHPA p33(tr), Photoshot/Moodboard p12(bcl);
Pixtal p25(forest); **Plain Pictures**/Westend61 pp5(br), 15(br),19(r),
25(br), 29(r), 35(br), 38(ml,mr), 65(br), 69(r), 72(bl); **Pitts Rivers**
p10(cl); **REX**/Brian Harris p11(tl), REX/Tony Kyriacou p11(c), REX/
Julian Makey p70(bl), REX/Sipa Press p76(tcm), REX/SIPA USA-
KT/SIPA p35(cl), REX Features/WestEnd61 p13(cr); **Science and
Society**/NPG p6(tr); **Science Museum**/Science and Society
p70(bcr); **Superstock**/Fancy Collection p22(cycling), Superstock/
Tetra Images pp12(tl), 77(cl); **Thinkstock** pp14(7), 24(3),
Thinkstock/istockphoto pp4(2-8,10), 5(bl), 9(l,r), 15(bl), 25(bl), 28(b),
29(l), 35(bl), 38(r), 64(9), 65(cl,bl), 69(l), 77(tr), Thinkstock/Photodisc
p20(6), Thinkstock/Pixland p13(cl), Thinkstock/Ingram Publishing
p70(tcl).
Commissioned Photography by Stuart Cox; pp2(c), 3, 4(c), 5(t),
6(tm), 10(t, b), 11(t, b), 12(tm), 13(t, b), 14(t), 15(t), 16, 20(t, b), 21(t, b),
23(t, b), 24(t), 26, 30(t, b), 31(t, b), 33(tm, b), 34, 35(tm), 36, 40(b),
41(t, b), 42(tm), 43(tr, br), 44, 46, 49(tl), 50(tl, b), 51(tr, br), 52(tm),
53(t, b), 54(tl), p55(tm), p56, 60(tl, bm), 61(tr, br), 62(tm), 63(tr, br),
64(tl), 64(5, 8), 65(tm), 66(tm,1-4), 67(5-9), p70(tl), 71(tr, b), 72(tm),
73(tr, br), 74(tm, bcm, bl, bml, bmr, br), 75(tl, bcl, bm), 76(tm, bcl,
bcr, bl, bm, br), 79(br).
Thanks to Madeleine, Callum, Georgia, Laura, Isaiah and Trevor.

These materials may contain links for third party websites. We have
no control over, and are not responsible for, the contents of such
third party websites. Please use care when accessing them.

Printed and bound in Argentina